TRACKSIDE
in the
Albany, N.Y. Gateway
1949-1974
with Gerrit Bruins

by Len Kilian *and* Jim Odell

Copyright © 1998
Morning Sun Books, Inc.

All rights reserved. This book may not be reproduced in part or in whole without written permission from the publisher, except in the case of brief quotations or reproductions of the cover for the purposes of review.

Published by
Morning Sun Books, Inc.
9 Pheasant Lane
Scotch Plains, NJ 07076

Library of Congress
Catalog Card No. 98-066086

First Printing
ISBN 1-58248-010-9

Color separation and printing by
The Kutztown Publishing Co., Inc.
Kutztown, Pennsylvania

DEDICATIONS

To my wife Mary Merle, whose unending patience, support and indulgence in my railfanning and insatiable accumulating is constant.
Len Kilian

To my parents Albert and Catherine Odell, whose Sunday drives usually ended up by some railroad tracks, thus forming a lifelong fascination for trains.
Jim Odell

ACKNOWLEDGEMENTS

This book would not be possible but for the efforts and patience of one individual-Gerrit Bruins. His interest in recording and preserving these scenes for fellow enthusiasts fills this book and has graced others. We cannot thank him enough for that.

We must add our appreciation for several others who contributed to our work. Gardiner Cross of INK[2], provided the skill in computerized graphics which made our maps. Frank Doherty, a retired New York Central conductor and director of the Bridge Line Historical Society, shared a running commentary to the slides selected for the book which enhanced the story of NYC operations in Albany as only a professional railroader could. Jeff English, a noted authority on the Rutland Railway, lent Gerrit's photos of Rensselaer and Troy from his collection. Some of the artwork used in the book was provided from the archives of the Bridge Line Historical Society while more came from the collection of Doug Barron. We must also note the encouragement and patience of our worthy publisher, Bob Yanosey. Bob took a gamble on an unknown photographer and a very concise body of work from which to assemble a book. We think the gamble paid off! Finally we must give a special thanks to the hundreds of unknown railroaders who allowed Gerrit to photograph their daily work. Without them Gerrit would not have had the material for the camera.

TRACKSIDE in the Albany, N.Y. Gateway 1949-1974

Gerrit Bruins Biography	3
The Albany Gateway	4
Albany	8
The Fulton Exposition	28
New York Central	33
Amtrak	74
Delaware & Hudson	77
Miscellaneous and Equipment	120
The Troy Branch and B&M	125
Rutland in Rensselaer	127

TRACKSIDE
in the
Albany, N.Y. Gateway
1949-1974
with Gerrit Bruins

Gerrit Bruins

WHILE THE CONFLAGRATION KNOWN AS WORLD WAR I RAGED AROUND HIM, a little boy was becoming a life-long railfan. Born in Goes, Holland on June 30, 1911, Gerrit Bruins and his family moved to the Hague, Netherlands at the outset of the "Great War". In the background during those years was the constant rumble of heavy artillery, including the legendary "Big Bertha". Even the frequently reverberating booms, low flying airplanes and the trappings of war did not deter him from being fascinated with the steam dummies and trams operating around him. These included the trains running to the seashore town of Schcevevingin, also drawn by steam locomotives.

Soon Nicholas Bruins emigrated to the United States along with his wife and five children of whom Gerrit was the oldest. The family settled in Albany, NY, although Gerrit and his brother lived with his aunts in Castleton. He later attended schools in Colonie, when his father reunited the family at their new home on Sand Creek Road.

Many retail department store jobs followed during the 1920's. He was working as a "runner" for Montgomery Ward in 1929 when the Depression hit and like so many of his generation, what followed were tough times with no thought, or money, for film given to his first love; the trains and trolleys around the Albany area.

After a stint in the Civilian Conservation Corps in Dutchess County and work in yet another "New Deal" idea, the Works Progress Administration, Gerrit managed to again be employed in the retail field. This time he was employed by two of the largest department stores in Albany, namely The Whitney Co. and John G. Myers. Money was very tight and he could still only observe the rail activity around him without being able to record anything on film. He has always regretted this state of affairs but it was a common plight amongst almost all at that time.

In 1942 Gerrit was drafted into the US Army Air Corps and became a member of the Air Transport Command serving in the 53rd Ferrying Squadron. Most of the war years were spent at Prestwick, Scotland. Prestwick was the ending point of the vast air bridge built across the North Atlantic and saw a vast number of aircraft delivered to their fighting commands by the ATC. Thus began another "love affair" he never got over: the sight and very distinctive sound of the big bombers. It continues to this day. Probably the saddest aspect of this job was his growing realization that not all "his" crews returned from their missions over Europe.

Gerrit contributed in his own small way to the success of the Big Three conference in Yalta. Enroute to his meeting with Churchill and Stalin, FDR stopped off at Prestwick enroute. As one would expect, the arrival of the Commander in Chief was greeted with full pomp and ceremony. Amidst all the brass Corporal Bruins was given the vital mission of custodial care for Fala, the Presidential Scottie. Alas, no photographic record of this part of the summit meeting seems to have been made.

With his Honorable Discharge in 1945, Gerrit returned to Albany to resume his life just like thousands of other GI's. Two important things then commenced, namely a twenty-three year long career at the Albany Veterans Hospital in housekeeping and maintenance and a serious desire to photographically record the rapidly changing railroad scene.

Gerrit never married, so he was able to pursue his avocation with no restrictions. Although he initially worked with black and white film, he was an early convert to color. In 1946 he started with a "Voightlander" camera taking postcard size photos. He then purchased a Leica M-3 and starting taking color slide images with a passion. Gerrit became an active member of the Capital District Railroad Club and participated in many fantrips sponsored by them. He also became an active member of the Mohawk and Hudson Chapter of the National Railway Historical Society and shared in their many excursions. An automobile was a luxury he could never afford and consequently he concentrated on areas and subjects that he could access by public transportation or, more often, by walking. This provided first hand experiences concerning the end of electric traction and early bus conversions as well as railroad subjects.

Unfettered by family or home responsibilities, he soon became a "regular" at Union Station and environs in downtown Albany. A forty year photographic idyll had begun. Although interested in all aspects of the varied railroad scene, his real love was always the passenger train and, in particular, the passenger cars of all types. From Pullmans to the off-line run through equipment, they all drew his attention. Very little escaped his documentation and fortunately that included photos of complete trains and support facilities. In those tolerant days, he was rarely bothered or harassed by railroad security personnel. This enabled him to obtain photo perspectives not available to the railfan photographers today. Although he indulged in occasional excursions and railfan trips, almost all of his time was spent in and around Albany.

The United Traction Company, by this time converted to buses, enabled him to record Delaware and Hudson action as far as the northern suburbs such as Menands, Watervliet and Cohoes. Fortunately he did not ignore engine servicing facilities at Colonie shops, on the B&M in Troy, or the quickly evolving Rensselaer facilities of the New York Central. He was out in all kinds of weather with no apparent regard for personal comfort. Summer, Fall, Winter or Spring were all the same to him. He lamented the passing of steam power and in particular the loss of most of the passenger trains. Eventually he made his peace with Penn Central, Conrail and Amtrak and was there to put them on film as well. Like all of us, he realized change was constant and inevitable because of the changing American travel habits. His father, a piano tuner by trade, was also a very accomplished painter of watercolors, some of which have survived. Perhaps this explains Gerrit's penchant for being in the right "spot" for the perfect image by showing a definite artistic flair.

Come with us then, as we enjoy the fruits of his efforts. A rare treat that we are very pleased to present to you here for the first time.

THE ALBANY GATEWAY

HISTORY

Someone once said that the key to success was "Location, location, and location". If so, Albany grew and prospered as a result of its placement on the North American continent. Penetration of the landmass required the use of waterways for transportation. The mighty North River was soon renamed the Hudson after an English adventurer in Dutch employ, allowed European access into the continent's interior for almost 170 miles before the end of ocean navigation. Most of that journey was through a gap in a series of ancient mountain ranges that we now know as the Catskills. Overland transportation was severely limited until a gap in the mountains emerged conveniently close to the limits of navigation. A second large river merged into the North River after falling over a tall waterfall that the natives called Cohoes. The original inhabitants of the region had long used this gap for passage to the west. The Europeans eventually named this western river the Mohawk in honor of the local Indian tribe. The Mohawk allowed movement west toward the Great Lakes. While navigable by canoe or bateaux, it was not a riverway suitable for heavy commercial traffic. The northern portion of the Hudson featured similar limitations. Portage was possible between the Hudson, Lake George and Lake Champlain drainages but this limited the volume of traffic able to be handled effectively.

European settlement followed upon the heels of European exploration. The Dutch opened a fur trading post close to where Henry Hudson had anchored while finding the head of navigation on the river. Initial contact with native populations was made in 1604. At about the same time, French explorers had penetrated as far south as Lake George. During the next eighty years, commerce and settlement slowly expanded until the arrival of the English. At the conclusion of a series of short but sharp wars between England and Holland, the English crown secured control of all of the settlements along the Atlantic coast. A royal charter was issued in 1686, formally changing the name of the original Dutch settlement on the North River from Fort Orange to Albany. The city retained much of its Dutch flavor until well after the Revolution, but grew as a gateway for English colonization of lands to the west and north. It served as a strategic post of supply during the final contest between the French and English crown and was the launching point for two expeditions against Quebec. Albany also served as the location for the first statement of common interest between the English colonies in North America and the royal government at home.

Albany continued in its role as gateway for expansion westward through the Revolutionary War period. It again acted as point of concentration for the campaigns leading up to Saratoga and the relief of Fort Stanwix (at present-day Rome). New England soldiers moved west after the war, pausing to buy final supplies in Albany. The initial stream of European colonists moving into western New York and the Mid-West stepped off their ships in Albany to start their trek. Rapid expansion west to the frontier and the necessities of national defense in the War of 1812 caused post war investment in transportation. The state of New York, under the leadership of Governor Clinton, took the revolutionary step of constructing a canal from the head of navigation on the Hudson River to the Great Lakes. Opened in 1823, the Erie Canal became a major route in the movement of settlers and immigrants to the west and the return of their products to the growing cities of the East. It established New York City as one of the leading ports in the world. It also spurred Albany's growth as an economic power, as all trans-shipping from canal to the river occurred on its doorstep. The region began to boom, with lumber and grain from the west meeting the finished products of the east. Albany supplied many of these products while other local cities, especially Troy, emerged as industrial centers as well. Troy quickly became a fierce rival to Albany and featured growing iron and steel manufacturing as its strength.

EARLY TRANSPORTATION

While location had helped the region's development, it still played a limiting factor on its growth. So long as water was the primary mode of transport, movement was limited by the change in elevation between the tidal Hudson and the Mohawk going west. The Erie Canal had tamed the great falls in the Mohawk at Cohoes by building a flight of locks around the falls at Waterford. This flight of locks, although an engineering marvel of the day, remained the choke point in the movement of traffic. Canal transport was cheaper, but still limited to the top speed of a team of mules.

Technology offered a solution to the problems of both speed and tonnage in the form of steam propulsion. Robert Livingston had demonstrated the improvements available through the use of steam on the river with the demonstration of his steamboat *Clermont* as early as 1805. By 1825 and the opening of the Erie Canal, steamboats were common on the Hudson and some were even taking note of the effect of harnessing steam to rails in England. Both canal and river transport were still seasonal in nature. It became evident that the use railroads was a possible solution to the problem of the canal locks. George William Featherstonhaugh of Duanesberg had the dream of using this new technology to avoid the delays of the Erie Canal. Less than two months after the opening of the canal he petitioned the state legislature for a charter for just such a railway. On March 29, 1826, the charter was granted and by 1830 the ground was broken. On August 13, 1831, the inaugural run on the 15.875 mile long Mohawk and Hudson Railroad steamed into history. The railway era in New York had begun.

In 1833, the legislature allowed the new railway to carry freight-but only during the season in which the Erie Canal was closed. Railroad building began in earnest, with the next link westward chartered as the Utica & Schenectady on April 29, 1833. By mid-summer of 1836 the two railways had joined together to operate the first through service between Albany and Utica. By 1843 there were a total of twelve pioneer railway companies in service between Albany and Buffalo advertising a single joint service. In 1844 the legislature reluctantly recognized the end of the state's monopoly on freight traffic by allowing the railroads to carry freight. It would take three years more before the legislature allowed this freight traffic to be conducted year round. Despite massive improvements in the Erie Canal in 1848, its era of transport supremacy was over. The Gateway remained, but it was made of iron rails.

NEW YORK CENTRAL

The Mohawk & Hudson's management had seen this change coming and recognized that their original route, which included the use of inclined planes at either end of the line, could not carry freight efficiently. They relocated their alignment to run up Patroon Creek along the side of West Albany Hill. On September 30, 1844, they began the daily assaults upon this hill by railroad trains that continue to this day. Albany's role as the railway gateway to the west went unchallenged until the New York and Erie reached Dunkirk, NY, in 1851. This forces the issue long discussed among the various companies and they petitioned the state for merger. On April 2, 1853, the legislature gave approval to the merger and the final contracts were penned on July 6, 1853. A new company, the New York Central, emerged under the leadership of Erastus Corning of Albany. It emerged as the largest railroad company in the United States with 297 miles of lines and 154 locomotives. Its acceptance in the marketplace was immediately evident. In the two years between 1854 and 1856 ton-miles increased by over 100%. The era of the slow moving passenger packet was over.

Early rail activity near the junction of the Mohawk and Hudson Rivers was not restricted to the railway of the same name. Financial powers in Troy also saw an opportunity to profit from a speedy way around the Erie's locks. The Rensselaer and Saratoga Railroad began its growth in 1832, laying track from Troy across Green Island up to the Spa City. One advantage in their route was the authorization to build the first rail bridge across the Hudson River. Another line moved along the course of the Mohawk River through Cohoes to Schenectady. The Schenectady and Troy merged into the New York Central but never enjoyed the advantages of the combination. Schenectady city fathers saw the light, also, and backed the construction of the Schenectady and Saratoga to the north. Similar lines moved eastward to connect with the great public works crossing the Berkshires. The Albany and West Stockbridge laid track east from Greenbush to meet the Western Railroad near Canaan. Troy interests supported the Troy and Boston, a line which eventually merged into the Fitchburg once the Hoosac Tunnel was opened.

By 1851, with the arrival of the Hudson River Railroad in what is now Rensselaer, the rail network through the Albany Gateway was complete but for two links. The line southwest into the Southern Tier and the connections with the Pennsylvania coal fields would wait for another fifteen years for the completion of the Albany and Susquehanna. A physical connection between the east and west banks of the Hudson at Albany would not be complete until the opening of a wooden Howe truss bridge in 1866. The completion or lack thereof, played a pivotal role in the consolidation of the New York Central and the Hudson River Railroad. The preeminent railroad magnate of the day-Commodore Vanderbilt-controlled the Hudson River Railroad. In addition to his control of that railroad and a massive fleet of steamships, the Commodore had invested in a number of other railroads, including the New York Central. In 1864 he used his considerable influence to back one side in a management struggle for control of that railroad. After

some financial maneuvering, the faction led by Erastus Corning and Dean Richmond entered into a treaty with the Commodore. This brought two years of relative peace and the opportunity to finally bridge the Hudson. Richmond's death in 1866 opened the door to the anti-Vanderbilt faction and a group headed by William G. Fargo (yes, that Fargo!) removed Vanderbilt's representation on the Board. The Commodore waited for his chance.

Three days after Christmas the Commodore had his opportunity as a great snowstorm descended upon Albany. By nightfall eight trains were snowbound in West Albany. The river had frozen over halting all ferry traffic. Vanderbilt waited until January 14 and then announced the abrogation of all through traffic agreements between his Hudson River Railroad and the New York Central. Central management was not prepared for the disruption in service that followed and was not sufficiently adept enough at public relations to avoid the blame for the resulting chaos. The State Legislature, a commodity frequently traded on Wall Street during this era, opened an inquiry that was hostile to Central management. Realizing the error of their decision, the Central's management invited the return of Vanderbilt interests to the Board that November. The official creation of the New York Central and Hudson River Railroad followed shortly-thereafter under Vanderbilt control.

Albany's role as Gateway continued unchecked until World War One. In 1873 the railroad opened a new double tracked bridge over the Hudson in Albany near Maiden Lane and the next year the railroad opened its first stretch of four-track main line between Schenectady and Utica. The West Albany Shops were expanded from their original M&H facilities into a major locomotive and car repair complex for the entire system. West Albany-built locomotives included the speedster #999. By 1898 the company recognized that the station facilities were overwhelmed by traffic and began construction on a magnificent new structure. The new Union Station was opened to traffic on December 17, 1900. It served trains radiating in every direction of the compass, with D&H service north and southwest, Central service on the main-line, B&A service to Boston and the recently acquired New York, West Shore and Buffalo providing routes along the west side of the Hudson. All of the passenger and freight traffic of the railroad converged to climb up or descend the Gateway over the troublesome West Albany Hill. Freight yards and locomotive facilities dominated the Rensselaer side of the river. As the Great War approached, NYC management started planning ways to break through the growing bottleneck in light of the growing flood of traffic.

Those plans came to fruition after the government returned operation of the railroads to the private companies at the end of the war. The Central planned to avoid the hill entirely by building a great by-pass around the Capital District. Using the West Shore RR as the starting point for construction, the railroad threw a great steel bridge across the Hudson near Castleton and built a large classification yard in the village of Selkirk, about fifteen miles southwest of Albany. In the process it upgraded the lines leading toward South Schenectady and Rotterdam Junction and high-speed cutovers were added in Guilderland and in Hoffmans, on the Mohawk River, to allow the movement of trains from one line to another. Connections on the East Side of the river were created to reach the Hudson Division at Stuyvesant and the B&A at Post Road. It required a grand total of twenty-five million dollars to complete the job. The investment paid for itself quickly, as freight traffic was largely routed off West Albany Hill. The B&A roundhouse in Rensselaer was closed by 1936 and further savings achieved by reducing the need for freight pushers on the Hill. The changes reduced traffic on this line, but reinforced the Albany region's role as Gateway as the new yard in Selkirk became the Central's Gateway to New England and the metropolitan New York area. It continues to serve in this important role to this day.

The use of Albany as a Gateway between New England and Pennsylvania was not as crucial or significant as its role in opening the West. Nonetheless, it was the only direct land connection for a number of years. The Western Railroad was the first to push tracks through the Berkshires. By the mid-1840s passengers and freight were making a relatively quick transit from the port of Boston to the shore of the Hudson River. The Boston & Albany route quickly attracted the bulk of the business going into and out of Boston itself. Traffic to Boston and points in northern New England moved north of the city of Albany, consolidated under the eventual control of the Boston & Maine. While considerable westbound traffic from the B&M joined the Water Level Route at Rotterdam Junction, NY, an alternative to a Central route was opened under the auspices of a rather unusual business enterprise- a company that started as a canal.

ALBANY CIRCA 1950

DELAWARE & HUDSON

Traffic moving directly north from the Albany-Troy area had been the early target of the Rensselaer and Saratoga. This line began a series of consolidations and expansions during the early days of railway growth and emerged as a strong regional carrier by the start of the Civil War. With the booming economic growth experienced immediately after the war, the R&S was able to secure its route along Lake Champlain to Plattsburg and connections to Montreal. In 1870, it became the target for takeover by the Delaware & Hudson Canal Company. The D&H canal had featured gravity railroads and anthracite coal mines as part of its own steady growth. The company recognized the need for expanded markets for its anthracite as well as the need to find a cheaper and quicker year-round mode of transportation. The post Civil War years offered the opportunity to tie a system together using both modes of transport.

RENSSELAER CIRCA 1950

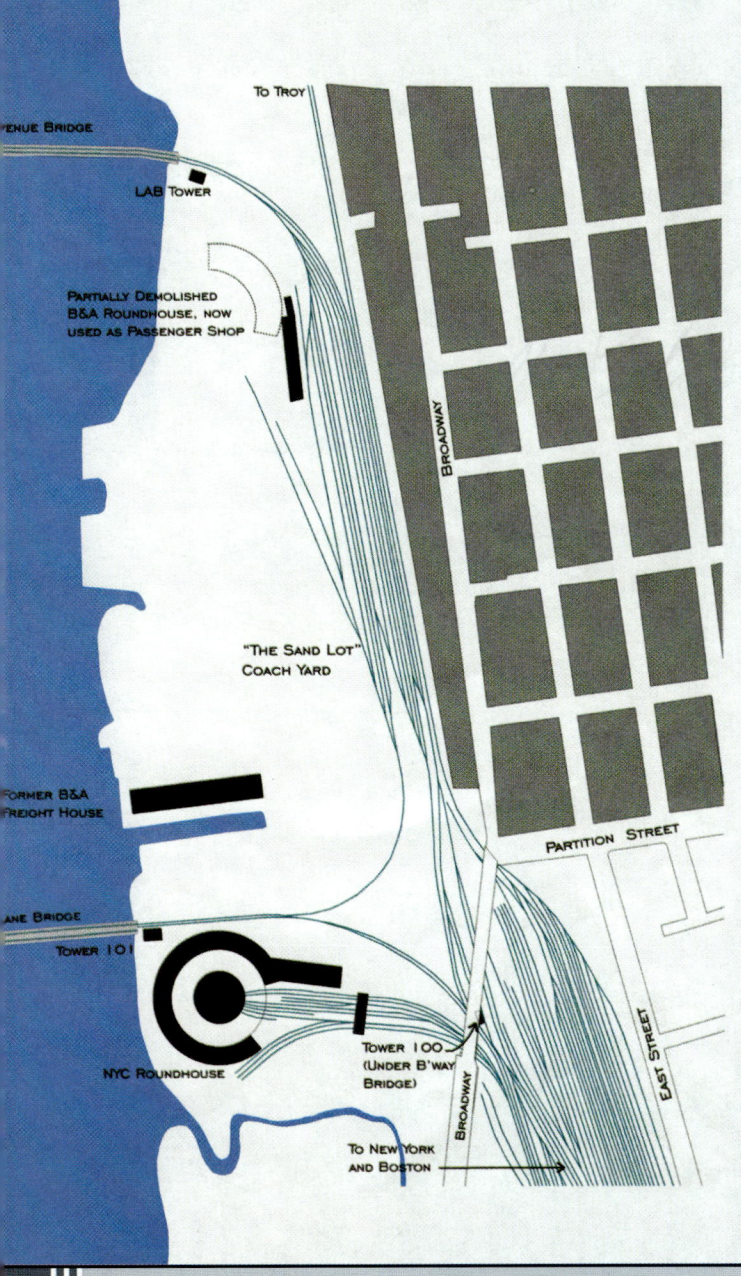

The Gateway between Albany and Pennsylvania took solid shape in 1860. A feeder line designed to siphon westbound traffic from the Central and to connect to the southwest was chartered under the name of the Albany and Susquehanna Railroad. Constructed to the standards of the broad-gauge Erie, the A&S built through the hills southwest of Albany into Schoharie County. It gradually tied rural communities such as Cobleskill, Oneonta, Unadilla, Sidney and Bainbridge into the transportation nets of Binghamton and Albany. Opened for traffic over its full length in 1866, the A&S quickly attracted the attention of the financial sharps then fighting the wars for control of the Erie. James J. Fisk and others saw the advantages of adding the A&S into the Erie system and moved aggressively to gain control. Albany forces reacted almost as quickly in a fight that moved from the legislature to the courts. Both sides invested time, effort and substantial contributions of money. Fisk appeared to be losing the legal battle, so he dispatched his forces out of Binghamton to physically control the railroad and install officers favorable to his bidding. The Albany forces retaliated by evicting these Erie men and a battle was joined just outside of Tunnel, NY, in 1869. Both sides had loaded their loyal sons of Erin onto trains that met in what has to be one of the wildest barroom brawls ever seen in New York State. The Albany forces gained local advantage, only to see the fight end with the arrival of armed militia units dispatched by the governor. The A&S was operated for a total of six months under militia orders while the state courts figured out the legal complications. The Albany forces won the court battle and ended the issue by leasing the A&S to the Delaware & Hudson Canal Company. The jewel had been stolen from right under the nose of the Erie. Before 1870 was over the Canal Company had added the R&S to its portfolio. The Delaware & Hudson Railroad as we knew it was now largely complete and in place.

TODAY

While the nature of traffic changed and the volume shifted, Albany continues to be a Gateway between East and West and between Canada and the United States. The colors of the New York Central faded, fell and arose as Penn Central, only to fall and arise again as Conrail. The corporate identity is expected to change again into CSX before 1998 is over. Regardless of corporate name, traffic still flows over the Selkirk line. Amtrak continues to fight gravity on West Albany Hill. The D&H changed, too, with Guilford arriving and receding, and the Canadian Pacific taking control by buying its way south. While it future is somewhat more in question, indications at the time of writing (1998) are that trains will continue to roll through the Albany area as they always have.

The Gateway captured by Gerrit in the following pictures was transitioning from the standard era of railroading into a period of decline and change. In a way, it matches the fate of the cities served by the railroads. They suffered decline and change. Like the railroads, most of the cities were considered dinosaurs that would eventually merge into vast beltways. Both the railways and the cities have surprised their critics and are showing signs of resurrection. Gerrit recognized the change and did his best to record its effect on railway passenger service. These photos present an epoch now past. A sharp eye, a good lens and film from Rochester captured many of the common things that made up the daily operations of railroads in the mid-twentieth century. We hope you enjoy them as much as we have.

ALBANY

Looking east from the tower of the A. E. Smith Building, the tallest structure in 1950 Albany, we look over the Hudson Valley into the hills of Rensselaer County. At the extreme left stands the Central Warehouse. Using its concrete bulk as our left guide, we look towards the right at the Livingston Avenue Bridge and, on the eastern or Rensselaer side of the Hudson, the old freight main line, the Troy branch and the passenger car yards. Just on this, the west side of the Hudson, lies the New York Central's Bull Run Yard. Also visible just above the buildings are the yards and passenger sheds of Albany Union Station. The station building is seen on the right side of the photo, emerging just beyond the copper roof of the State Court of Appeals Building.

Our view now shifts to almost directly east. Bracketed between the red towers of the State Capitol lies State Street. The classic Delaware and Hudson Building, topped by its statue of Hudson's *Half Moon*, rests at the foot of the State Street Hill. The building is just north of the original Dutch settlement of Fort Orange and lies where tradition says Henry Hudson first set foot in the area. Just above the left tower of the Capitol is the Maiden Lane Bridge. Just to the right of the bridge, across the Hudson, is the roundhouse and servicing facilities of the New York Central. You can see how the passenger main crosses the Hudson; swings passed the roundhouse and turn south, but railroad east, toward New York City, 163 miles down the Hudson River. The Boston & Albany angles southeast, climbing up the hill to eventually join the freight main at Post Road, 12 miles away.

Often mistaken for the State Capital, the D&H's Plaza complex fills the area at the foot of State Street reputed to be Henry Hudson's original landing site. The three buildings were constructed at the behest of the D&H and several civic leaders starting in 1912. The original D&H portion includes the northern or left wing and the tower. Company officials soon realized that more space was needed and instructed Albany architect Marcus Reynolds to mirror the lateral wing. The southern most building that completes the facade was constructed as the editorial offices of the *Albany Journal*. The Plaza served as a junction for most of the electric railway routes into Albany. Gerrit captured this photo which shows that the Plaza continued in that role well into the introduction of busses. The building eventually became the headquarters of the State University of New York and, at time of publication, is completing an extensive period of refurbishment.

(Above) The centerpiece and ground zero for our tour of the Albany Gateway is Albany Union Station, shown here in June 1960. Opened on December 17, 1900, this was the third and most grand of New York Central stations to serve Albany. Its upper level tracks saw the pride of the Great Steel Fleet connecting travelers to Chicago, Toronto, St. Louis, Pittsburgh and the American heartland. The lower or street level tracks served a more mundane patronage headed for Weehawken by way of the West Shore and Montreal or Binghamton by way of the Delaware and Hudson. Its upper floors served as offices for the railroad and its lunchroom fed countless travelers for over sixty years. The station also served a variety of bus lines for both city and suburban routes. The station was closed on December 28, 1968 and reincarnated after almost 20 years as the operations center for Northstar Bank, now Fleet Bank.

Let's start in Rensselaer at the roundhouse. We are looking roughly northwest at some time prior to 1954. The Hudson shows some hard service but has traded its original tender for a PT-type pedestal or centipede type. The EMD F-7A freight units had most likely dropped down the Hill from West Albany for service. The round-roofed building behind the diesels was a Boston & Albany freight house. It had seen much busier days before the Selkirk Branch opened in 1927 and rerouted freight traffic off the Albany hill.

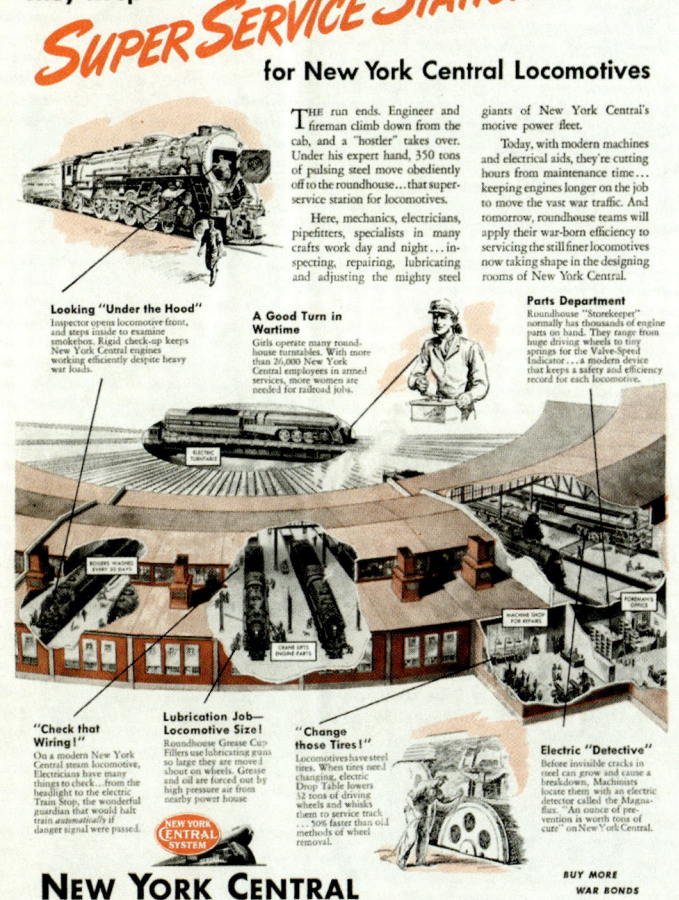

The centerpiece for steam facilities in Rensselaer was the coaling tower. The hoppers on the left dropped coal into a hopper in the shed. The coal was lifted by conveyor to the top of the bunker above the service tracks. Sand was loaded and dispensed on the right side of the bunker. During the mid-1970's, this structure had to be removed to make way for the construction of a new high school. Several contractors found out just how strong the concrete was. They tried time and time again to knock down its legs with explosives, only to watch as the dust cleared to show the tower still standing. Eventually they won, but the cost was high.

If you look closely behind the J-3, you can see why those F-7's had stopped at the roundhouse. The coaling tower shares its sand with units which otherwise had no reason to stop there. The Central soon after this built a small diesel facility with fuel racks and sand tower behind the photographer. This simplified the process of servicing diesels, but still required West Albany units to make the trip down into the river valley. Note the maroon Chevy - probably the prized possession of an engineman.

(Above) Niagara 6023 (Alco, 1946) rests awaiting its next assignment. The boiler shows some signs of deferred maintenance, but the running gear shows that some care has been given to the 4-8-4 in preparation for further runs. Despite its rough look, this 6000-class engine represented the cream of NYC Steam power and provided a real test for its diesel competitors. The rusty discoloration appears on a number of photos of Niagaras of this period and may have been the result of leaks or discharges form near the pilot - perhaps from the front-mounted air pumps.

(Below) J-1c class #5251 (Alco, 1929), originally built for the Michigan Central, sits two tracks over from an unidentified 6000-type Niagara. Both are under steam and ready for assignment. Gerrit stepped just inside one of the roundhouse stalls to get a portrait of two famous locomotive types. As you can see, this roundhouse did not deal with mere freight power but stabled primarily Central passenger racehorses.

(Right) Gerrit gives a peak through the pedestrian fencing on the walkway across the Maiden Lane Bridge into the throat of the south end of the station's upper level. #6022 is ready to head east or south with a local for New York. One of the new General Motors E-8's, still shiny in its factory-fresh coat of paint, sits one track over, also ready to depart. The towerman in Tower A will be busy for a few minutes as these two trains start their journeys.

(Below) Gerrit repeated the view in July of 1961 with different machines. E-8 #4089 and its unidentified companion E-7B have a few more miles on it than its sister in the previous photo, but the action is about the same. The D&H is just peaking into the scene on the right as an RS-3 has brought up the through cars from train #34, THE LAURENTIAN.

(Right) Train #51, THE EMPIRE STATE EXPRESS, sits in front of Tower B, stretched well beyond the public platforms. The late morning departure allows a nice broadside sun on both units and train. The train was receiving the full attention of the shop forces as the trucks still shine in their original silver. Gerrit was standing at the throat of the coach yard in order to capture this full-length portrait.

(Above) RS-3 #8228 and a sister draped in passenger grey move slowly across the Maiden Lane Bridge to pick up their eastbound train. The fireman seems rather casual about the move. Gerrit remembers that he thought that perhaps the man had done this so many times before. It was back to business once the units rolled past Tower A.

(Right) An unidentified Hudson starts to move eastbound across the Maiden Lane Bridge for New York. Although the slide is undated, we suspect it was taken around 1950. The sight must have still been common, as the gentleman walking toward the photographer seems completely unconcerned about the show taking place above him. While the locomotive retains its original tender, it was modified to use Baker valve gear.

(Above) Gerrit looked north to capture this view of the coach yard on the upper level. Clearance Car X-8016 rests on one track while Pullman-operated sleepers *Poplar Borough* and *James Bay*, a 22-bedroom sleeper, await service alongside. X-8016 started life as a Brill gas electric and lived well into the diesel age working for the engineering department.

(Below) Gerrit's love for passenger cars caused him to keep an eye open for good car portraits. Pullman-owned but New York Central operated heavyweight *White Castle* caught his eye, but he also succeeded in capturing ice service refrigerator cars used to fill the ice bunkers of Pullman cars and coaches alike. The towers of the Livingston Avenue Bridge can be seen immediately behind the cars.

(Above) EMD SW-1 #585 moves three D&H coaches into position for attachment to their New York Central connecting train. The 585 wears a dark grey color which sometimes adorned passenger switchers. D&H coach 203 wears a fresh coat of Pullman green. This was a conservative change from its original 1939 World's Fair scheme of green and cream. Central switchers did all the work on the upper level and Gerrit caught the teamwork between the two roads which made this a Union Station.

(Below) EMD SW-1 #602 sits at the south end of the station for a classy portrait. The unit is nice and fresh and shows considerable attention from the paint shop for safety highlighting its handrails. The locomotive's crew, along with the conductor and brakeman assigned to the yard may well be taking a short break in the buildings behind the locomotive. These structures provided crew locker rooms, parts storage, track and car supplies and lubricating oils for the different cars and locomotives serviced in the station. They became known as "Tammany Hall", perhaps in deference to the Irish heritage of so many of the men. It is also possible that this may have been in reference to some of the railroad politics which no doubt took place therein.

19

(Above) You can almost feel the cold of this February 1962 day as power sits near Tower B. The E's may go to New York (Harmon) but that RDC1 will have to fight the snow over the Berkshire hills before it gets to Boston later this evening. While the Beeliners played a role in passenger operations in Albany their sound still reminded Gerrit of one of his other interests - busses.

(Below) Gerrit sought shelter from the snow later that day but traincrew and switchmen still had to brave the elements to get the job done. The crewman walking towards the photographer will be glad to enjoy some of the warmth of steam heat once his train is ready to depart.

(Above) The Boston RDC idles next to a standard coach that same February day while a set of D&H RS-3's pull their cars into a snowy station. The built-up snow around the couplings will make the work of exchanging power for NYC E units that much more difficult for the car knockers.

(Below) Changes in paint have no effect upon changes in weather. Gerrit caught this scene four years later in February 1966. The switch heaters are eating propane as they fight to keep the switch points free. The Central will be glad it has steam lines throughout the yard to keep its coaches warm and ready for service. Yard steam keeps water lines on the cars from freezing and avoids costly repairs, so the billowing steam is a sign that all is well.

(Above) On a much nicer day the upper level coach yard displays a variety of color schemes in this October 1963 shot. EMD SW-1 #594 is in switcher black while #4053 shows dirty lightning stripes and E-7A #4010 sports its new cigar band. The RDC's safety stripes add a dash of bright color to the greys.

(Below) The rains of May 1968 wash the cars of this Empire Service train. The New York Central introduced Empire Service in 1967 when it radically changed its levels of passenger service. Penn Central emerged on February 1, 1968 and continued the service. As can be seen, there were few initial changes to differ this Penn Central 3-car train from its earlier counterparts.

(Above) Another May 1968 Penn Central view and we see NYC #4054 lead three immaculate cars westbound past Tower A. The train appears to be running reversed main. The railroad tried to bring the trains in close to the main building for passenger convenience. Tower architecture varies as Tower A looks almost pagoda-like while the D&H Plaza tower is clearly Flemish Gothic.

(Below) Rail photographers gather in May of 1968 to catch the novelty of a Pennsylvania Railroad E-7B MU'ed with three New York Central E units as they roll across the western throat of the station. Tower B controls the movements of this train from the west. While it isn't identified on the slide this might well be train #428, the remnants of THE NEW ENGLAND STATES.

(Above) By May 1968 Penn Central was using freight units to operate some of its mail trains. Another Pennsy unit, a GP-35, splices a Central GP-40 and U28B, as the Boston-bound mail train backs down on its train after dropping a cut of cars. The art deco main post office had a direct connection with the platforms. Soon hordes of loaded mail carts will disappear into the maws of the building. Albany again demonstrates its contrasting styles of architecture.

(Right) Contrasting architectural style of locomotives is shown in these early Penn Central days as the square nose of a D&H PA stands in comparison with the bulldog nose of EMD E-8 #4052. The symmetry of the shed columns leads the eye to the end of the corridor, a baggage elevator and access to the subway connecting the platforms with the station.

(Above) We drop down to the lower level of the station to capture two Fairbanks-Morse road switchers resting alongside the Railway Express Building. 7006 and 7009 were delivered in July 1951 and spent time working a variety of local assignments on the B&A, the West Shore and the Hudson Division. The stream-style design of the FMs by Raymond Loewy complimented the curves of the Pontiac very nicely.

The Bull Run local, led by Alco S-2 #8576, gets ready to return its empties to West Albany in June of 1962. Bull Run saw a variety of local businesses use its team tracks. The D&H main line, seen in the foreground, appears to need some attention to its weeds. In contrast, the signal cabin in the foreground must have recently seen the brush of the Signal Department's painter.

(Left) SW-1 #590 leads several Pullmans over to the D&H for interchange. The cars, including the trailing SP-owned car, were probably in tourist or charter service. The mid-afternoon photo rules out any chance that the cars were being used in routine D&H trains.

(Right) Bull Run Yard made its share of contributions to the Central's mail and express revenue. A number of such cars, including a rider car on the tail end, await attention. While enthusiasts might pay closer attention to these cars or to the two styles of Pacemaker boxcars servicing Albany's less than carload traffic, our spectator seems to find the MG model "TF" more interesting.

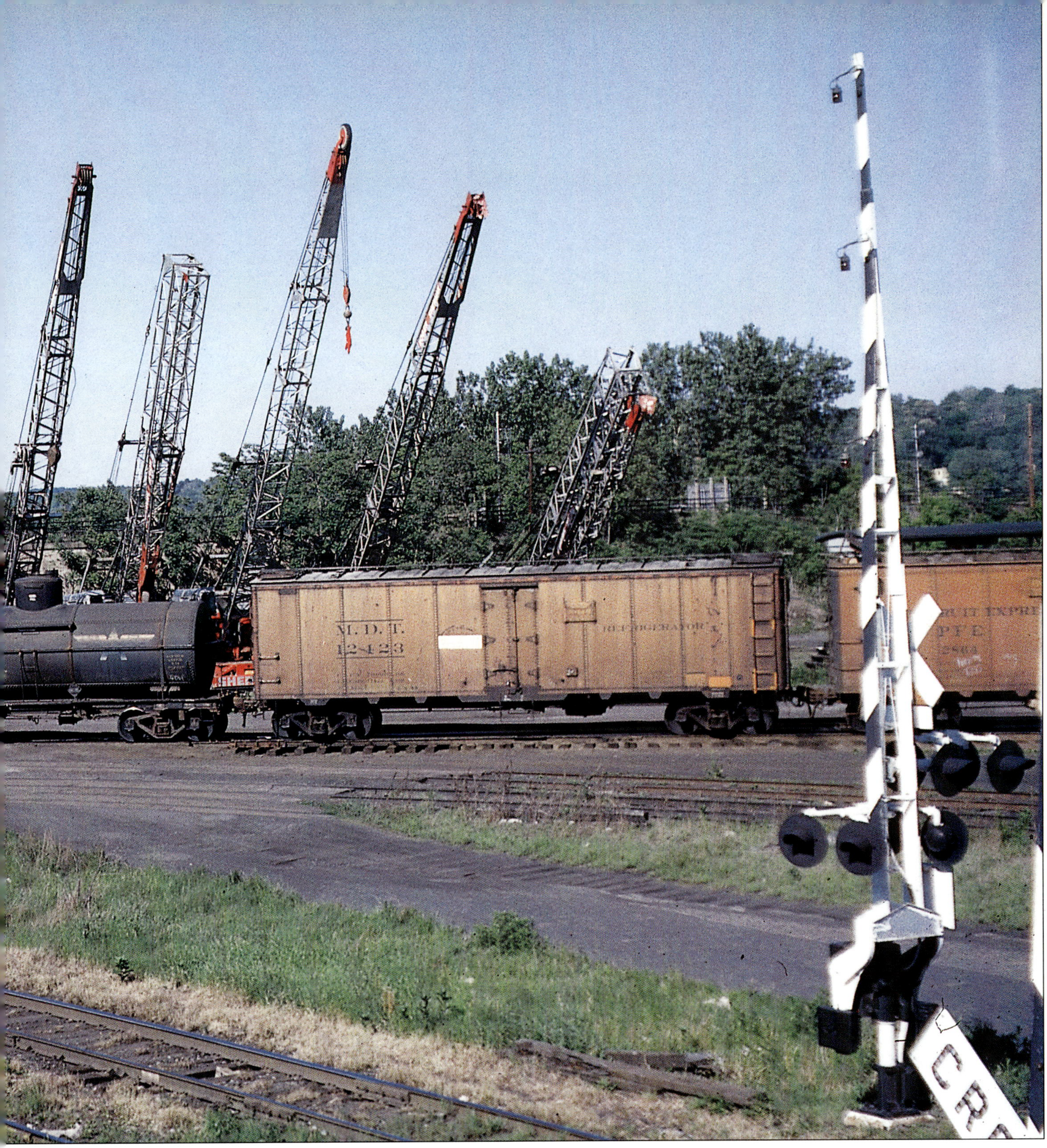
M.D.T.
12423
REFRIGERATOR

Pacemaker
FREIGHT SERVICE

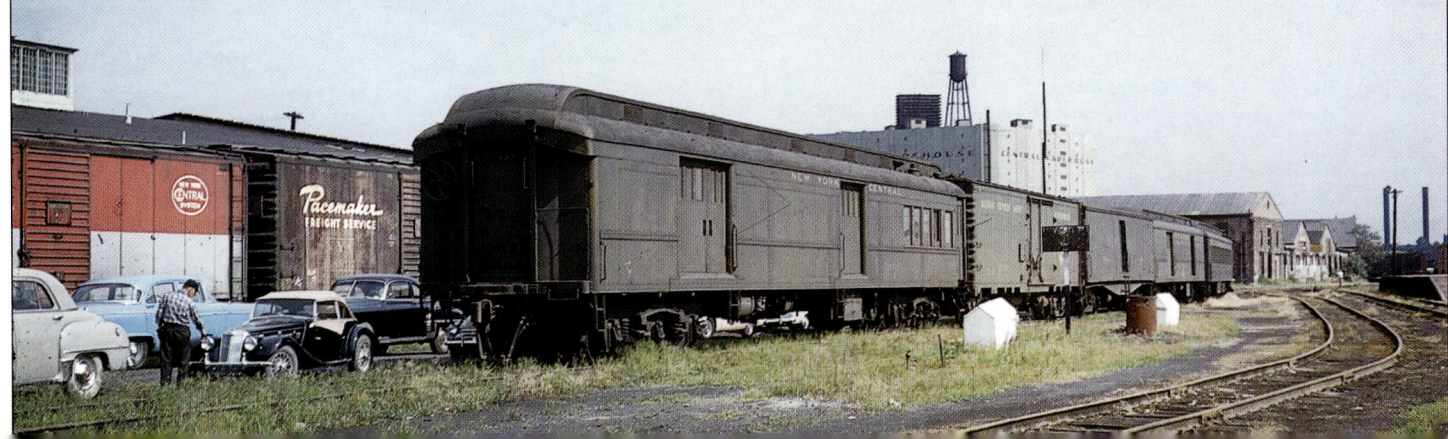

THE FULTON EXPOSITION

(Right) The afternoon sun provided the rich light and fluffy clouds as the backdrop for a portrait by Gerrit of E-8 #4040. The Central also displayed samples of Budd's art of stainless steel passenger car construction specially prepared for this display. The E unit shows one change made in its paint scheme for the sake of economy. The trucks have been repainted grey instead of the original silver. More such economies were only a few years away.

(Left, inset) In 1959 communities all along the Hudson River celebrated the Sesquicentennial of the introduction of steamboats to the Hudson. The Fulton Exposition was celebrated in Albany with, among other events, a display of railroad equipment sponsored by the Railroad Community of Eastern New York. The D&H and the Central hosted their portion of the display in Bull Run Yard that September. The star of the show was the much modified hero of the EMPIRE STATE EXPRESS, 4-4-0 #999.

(Above) The public has arrived and the flags and plaques have been spread out to cover the fact that 999's valve gear has been disconnected. These changes only shroud the more extensive mechanical changes made when the world's record holder was rebuilt in the West Albany Shops for more routine traffic.

(Below) The Central proudly demonstrated its latest entry into the intermodal portion of the transportation industry. This Flexi-Van platform sports a closed container and a rare open, or "rag top", container. Both were designed to meet the various requirements of the Central's shippers. The railroad operated a small Flexi-Van facility in Bull Run Yard through the mid-1960's. This facility also handled the bulk commodity side of the business-Flexi-Flo.

(Above) Earlier that year, in June, the New York Central displayed a number of its other modern freight cars. The display included 40 and 50-foot Century green boxcars, a mechanical refrigerator, a 70-ton capacity triple hopper, a Flexi-Van car and a coil steel car. Gerrit photographed the string of cars being moved along the back row of storage tracks on the upper level of the station. Central modelers will no doubt join us in wishing that Gerrit had a bit more interest in freight cars as well.

(Below) The Delaware & Hudson's contribution to the display included a recent rebuild. Car #35215 began life as a wood sheathed open platform coach sometime around the start of the century. It was modernized for local service between Carbondale and Wilkes-Barre, Pa. With the end of that service the car replaced another wood car as the company's Safety Instruction Car.

(Above) International Car Company got its first order for steel cabin cars from the D&H in 1959 after the legislature of the Commonwealth of Pennsylvania prohibited the use of wooden cars with pusher locomotives. #35713 proudly joined the display, sharing the spotlight with some new Trailer Train equipment.

(Below) Later that afternoon Gerrit returned to the upper level of Union Station to capture D&H Business Car 200 in newly applied gold striping. Other Sesquicentennial displays are seen in the background. Of particular interest is one of Alco's International series of locomotives. Based on the FA design, it sits on a flat car awaiting export to one of the broad gauge lines of the Indian subcontinent. Automobile enthusiasts will be as interested in these shots of the lower level for the views of the parking lots as modelers are for views of the railroad equipment.

NEW YORK CENTRAL

NEW YORK CENTRAL SYSTEM

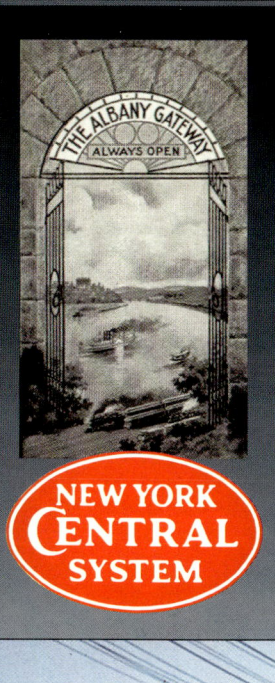

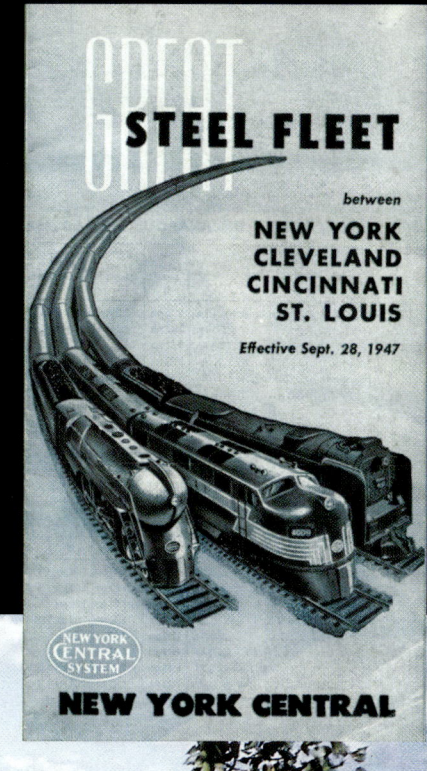

The Livingston Avenue Bridge sits center-on in this photo as one of the New York Central station switchers pushes a cut into the Rensselaer coach yards. Tower 100 in the background protected movements across the bridge. Although the Central's official designation for the structure was SS#100 (standing for Signal Station) most simply called it a tower. By October of 1959, when this photo was made, the Delaware and Hudson had changed its passenger colors to better match with its connection to New York. The Central's efforts at vegetation control are evident in the scorch marks made by the weed burner in a recent visit.

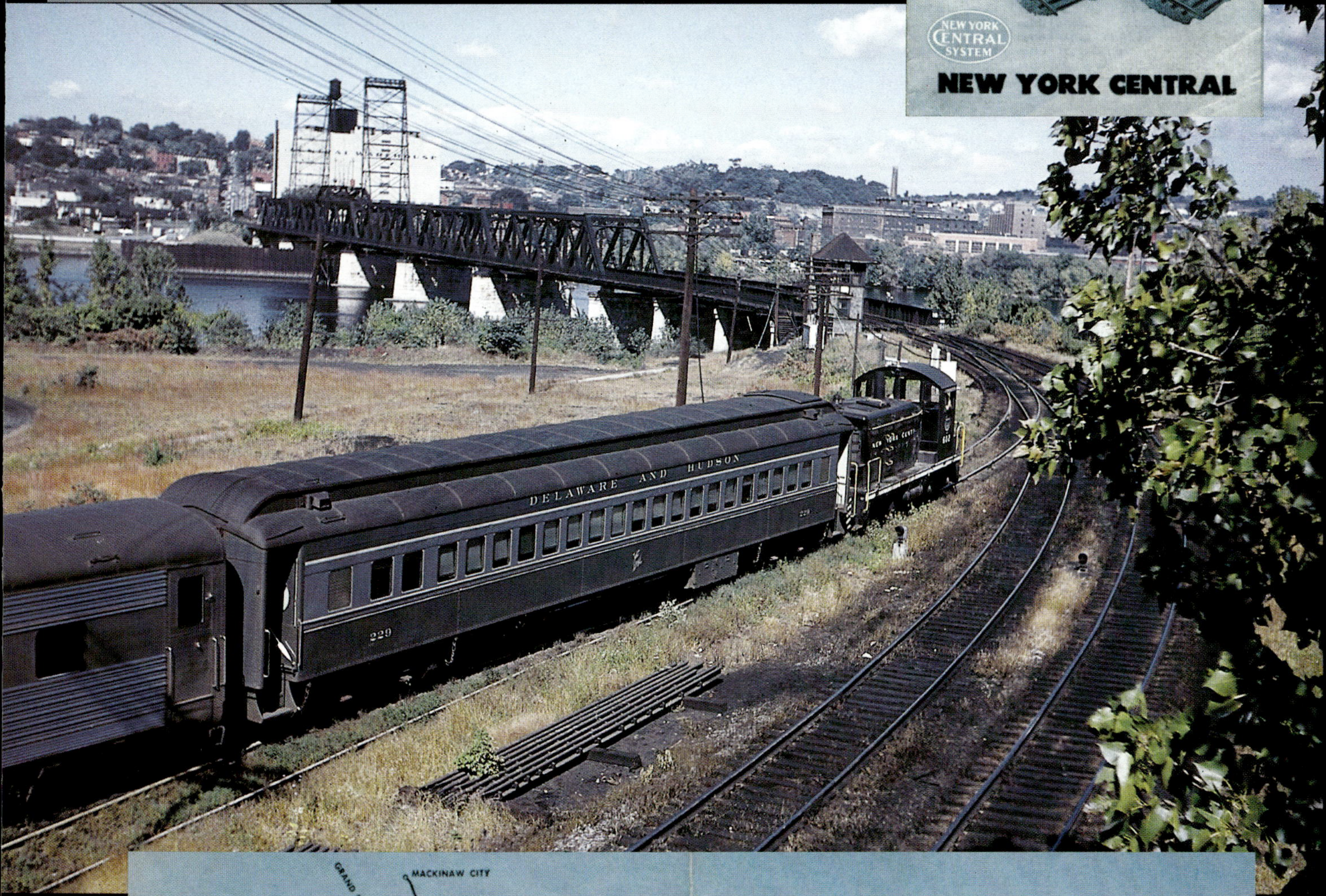

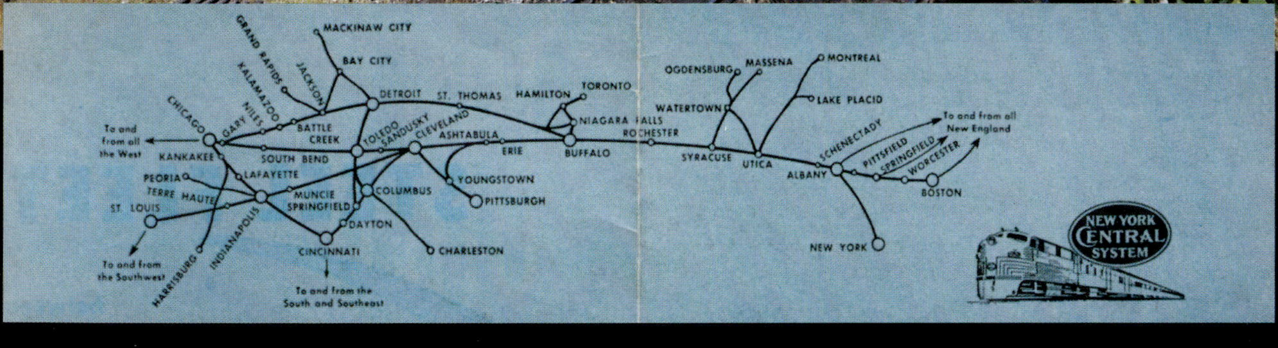

(Above) SW-1 #602 with its new-image herald pushes its cut past a steam generator car showing its readiness for service with a feather of steam. The car shops sit behind the generator car. Some of the work underway can be seen on the track behind the heater car as the shop force has jacked up the end of one car for better access to the trucks.

(Right) S-2 switcher #8521 drifts south past the Rensselaer coach yards under the watchful eyes of its engineer. The job's ground man, either its brakeman or conductor, seems to be enjoying his ride on the unit's back platform. You might notice his employee's timetable folded over in his pocket. The Central's light buff covers always im-proved visibility when they were held in the hand used to signal moves.

(Above) Looking south toward Tower 100, Gerrit captures the coach yard at the height of its business. Originally part of the B&A's freight yards, the passenger yards stored cars awaiting assignment. The yard is filled with heavyweights - Pullmans and coaches. A generation later this ground was again used for railroad maintenance as the Amtrak Rensselaer Maintenance Facility. If you look closely in the right of the background you can barely see the coaling tower of the steam facilities.

(Below) One of the Budd-built observation cars brightens up the coach yard despite its majority of drab standard cars. The local freight from Troy is passing by headed south. Things are changing and at least one housewife in Rensselaer is taking advantage of cinderless air to do her wash. Central crews referred to this yard as "the Sand Lot".

One bright but cold winter morning three FA's move toward the Livingston Avenue Bridge after receiving a clear semaphore indication from the operator of Tower 100. While the New York Central had the largest fleet of Alco FA's used by any railroad, they were still relatively rare on these tracks. Most freight operations by-passed Albany by moving through the classification and hump yard at Selkirk. The Central scheduled one freight to West Albany from DeWitt Yard in Syracuse and return. This train was AD19 and DA20. Once the shops in West Albany had closed, the freight power was sent down the hill to be fueled and serviced for the return to Syracuse.

(Right) A switchman opens a turnout for a cut of cars led by the Central's diesel instruction car and a milk car. Baggage and express equipment outnumbers passenger-carrying cars in this August 1958 photo. Those Pullman-Standard stainless steel coaches are definitely in the minority.

(Left) Two different switchers shuffle the deck in the yard as one pulls a sleeper while the other switches an RPO. By July of 1959, two-tone grey was finally being seen on the head-end cars, as we can see from the very dirty RPO sitting in front of Budd-built 10 bedroom 6 roomette *Peaceful Valley*. The track in the foreground was used by mail and express trains to by-pass Union Station while the line to Troy, seen on the far left, had been reduced to freight only since January of 1958.

(Above) An E-8 coupled to a 4100-class Alco PB eases a mail and express train past the backyards of Rensselaer's Broadway. The train is rolling through the outer series of interlockings which controlled movements across the wyes leading to the Maiden Lane Bridge, through the B&A crossing and south to New York. It looks like more housewives have recognized the transition from steam to diesel as they air their linens.

(Below) Some sort of "service interruption" must have forced a call for the wreck train. With the closing of the West Albany shops in the mid-1950's, this train probably made its roundabout way from Selkirk. The outfit includes wheel cars, crane #X-13, a boom tender, tool car and crew car. The crane's number seems somewhat indicative of its work; whenever it shows up to work somebody must have had bad luck.

(Above) In April of 1961, Alco S-1 #827 switches RDC-1 #M-461 toward the fueling pad. RDC's provided an active local service; connecting Albany to Boston and Poughkeepsie as well as operating commuter runs from Hudson and Chatham. As the services were eliminated, the cars were moved south and operated on the lower Hudson Division and on the Harlem Division.

(Below) In 1961 the New York Central sought simpler alternatives to its lightning stripe paint scheme. E-8 4052 enjoys the late September sun as it moves back toward Union Station. This was one of three units - two E-8's and an E-7B-painted in what some called jade green. The Central preferred to call the paint "Century Green".

(Above) Another power set rattles past Tower 100 late one afternoon in September of 1961. Alco PA-1 #4209's presence suggests its use on a secondary train. Despite their classy lines, the Alco passenger units never established a good reputation on the Central. Enginemen preferred to use the units in trailing position. They were all removed from service well before their contemporary competitors, the E-7's, ended their service lives.

(Left) One July morning in 1960 sees three RDC-1's move across the Troy leg of the wye heading for the fueling rack. These may have come north as Train #699 from Poughkeepsie. This train departed at 6:37 a.m. for Albany, making all stops in between. It would head south at 5:15 p.m. as Train #698, scheduled for a 6:54 p.m. arrival in P' town, where the units would layover for the next day. These locals did not survive the reductions in service that followed over the next few years.

(Right) Late one afternoon in July 1962, RS-3 #8240 and a caboose move a string of Pennsy head end cars north towards Troy. The caboose suggests this is not just a normal switch move. The PRR cars are end-door baggage cars of the type used in moving theatrical equipment or scenery. Similar cars were sold to the Ice Capades show and were often spotted in Troy's Adams Street freight yards while the shows used the ice of the RPI Field House. Perhaps Gerrit caught just such a move this day.

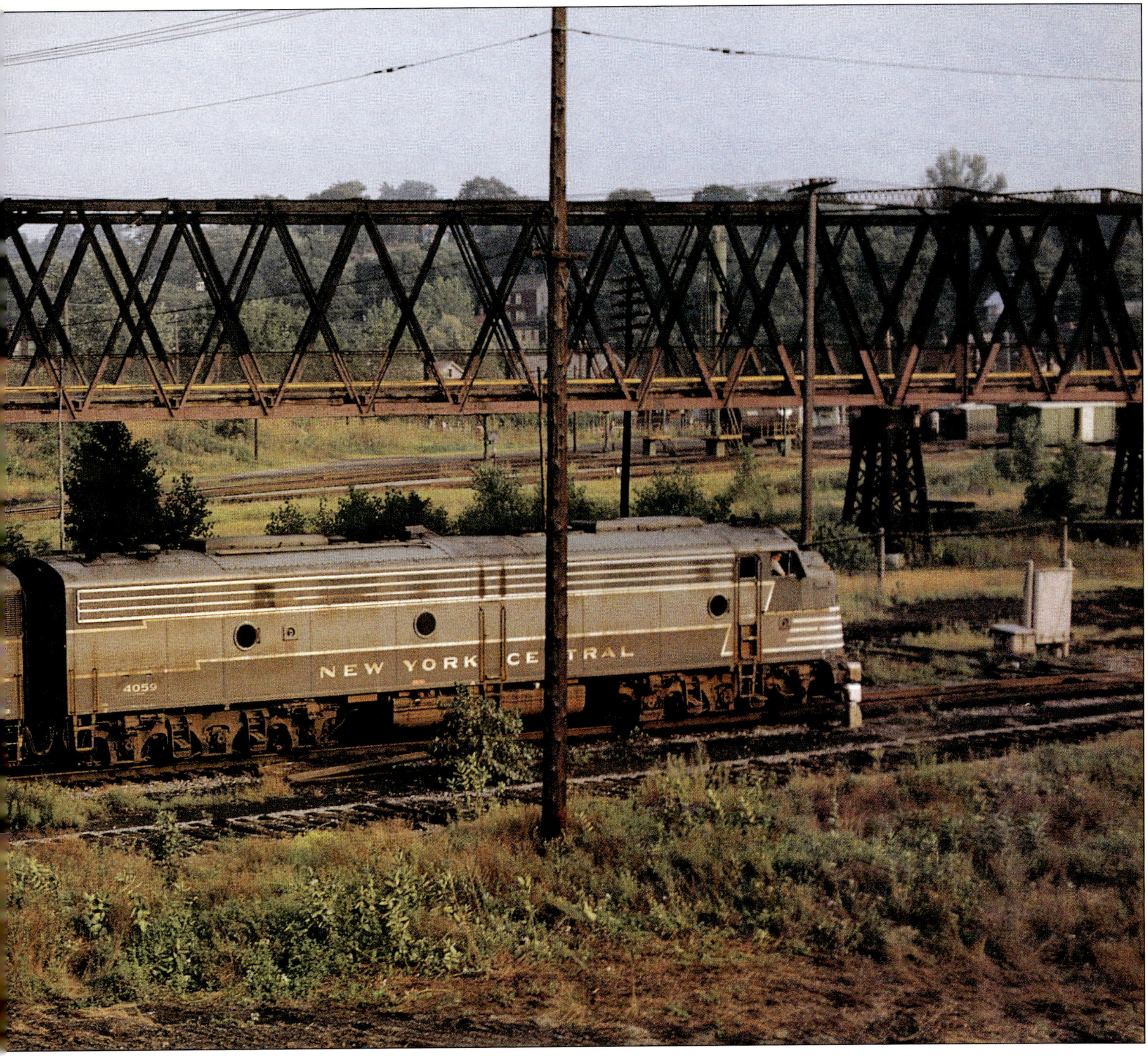
NEW YORK CE TRAL
4059

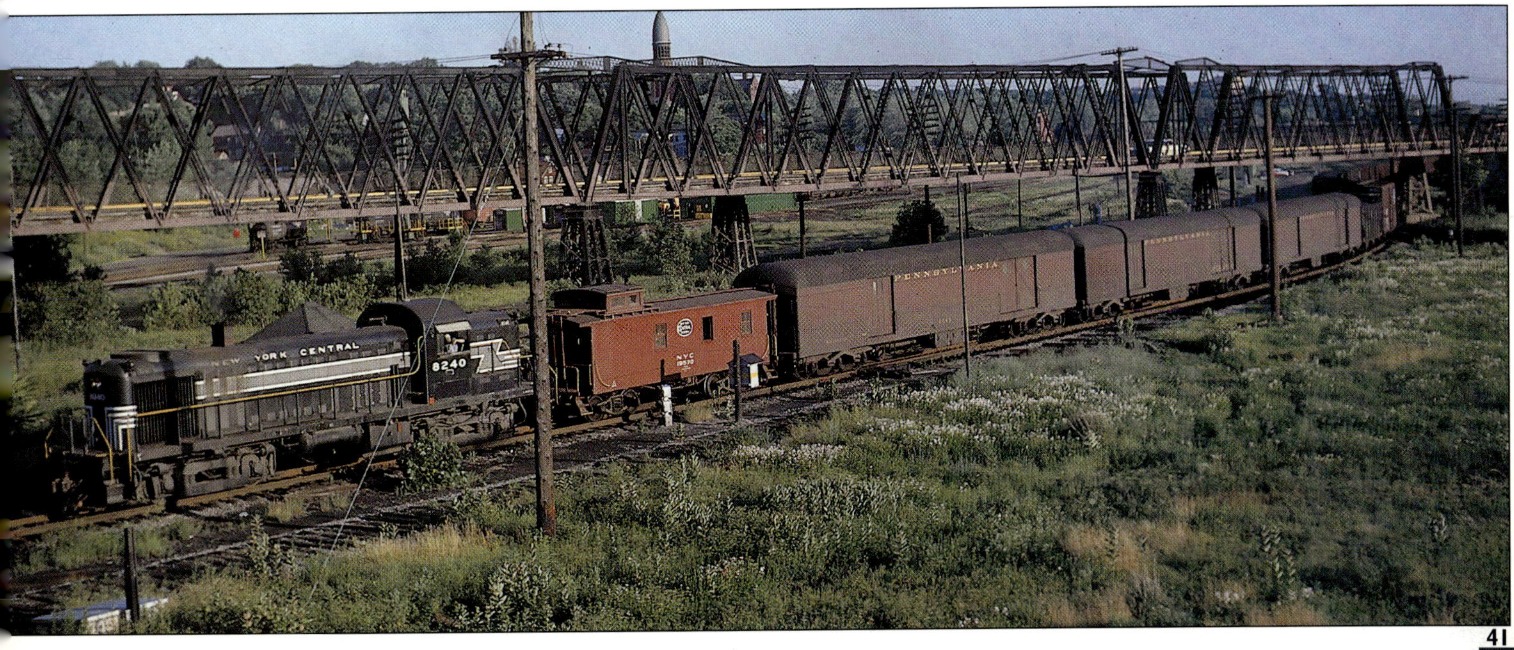
NEW YORK CENTRAL
8240
PENNSYLVANIA

On a July afternoon in 1961 two EMD E-8's move along the Troy leg of the wye. The requirement to fuel locomotive in Rensselaer and return them to Albany must have kept the operators in Towers 101 and 99 and the locomotive hostlers busy. The tracks shown in the photo have since been replaced by the Rensselaer High School.

(Left) Another power move-this time during the spring of 1957-catches a different set of road freight power heading for the service area. RS-3 #8261 pilots Fairbanks-Morse CFA-16 "C-Liners" #6605 and a sister. As with earlier photos, the units had probably come down the hill after powering a Syracuse-West Albany job.

(Below) Alco RS-3 #8315 heads north passed Tower 100 in March 1962. The unit is decorated in the new, simplified version of the "cigar band" paint scheme. It is returning to West Albany after serving local industries as far south as Castleton. The industry in Castleton, Brown Paper (now Fort Orange Paper), remains the only freight customer on this Conrail line at time of publication.

(Right) By the early Sixties, Central sought to reduce its passenger-related expenses by eliminating its famous lightning stripe scheme. The only question was what would be the new simplified (cheaper) paint scheme. Things usually don't turn green in October, but Gerrit caught E-8 #4053 accompanied by a more conventionally striped sister later that month. The coach yards and shops which once filled the background are now gone. The Sandlot is now empty. It would be almost another twenty years before rail tracks return to this site. It is now the home of Amtrak's Rensselaer Engine Facility.

(Left) October of 1961 saw two more versions of experimental paint schemes move across the wye. #4052 wears its cigar band herald a bit lower than its partner #4080. You can see that this paint scheme was getting closer to what would emerge as the final passenger scheme. It is close, but still no cigar!

(Below) Just about the same location, but in April of 1965, Gerrit caught #4047 turning on the wye. 4047's lettering and markings are in the positions that eventually were standardized as the grey scheme. But this test unit substituted gold instead of the white for lettering and marking. Although the gold was not selected, it certainly shows up much better than the heavily weathered companion still in lightning stripes.

45

It is April of 1968 and a mail train crosses the bridge for points east. By this time Flexi-Vans were being used almost exclusively for mail service. The Albany skyline is changing as the steelwork of the Agency Building is taking shape above the South Mall's stone walls. Entire neighborhoods were removed to make way for this new office complex. Albany, like it or not, was changing.

(Left) #4047 now sits on the lead to the Maiden Lane Bridge, giving Gerrit a chance to get a track-level portrait. Just above the steam generator vent you can see the top of the D&H's Plaza Building and the Half Moon statue on top. To the right is the white form of the Post Office Annex, the red roofs of the Capitol and the A.E. Smith building tower constitute the skyline. This would change over the next four years as Governor Rockefeller placed his mark upon Albany.

(Right) E-7A #4024 leads a string of Pullman-Standard and Budd coaches and sleepers into the late afternoon sun in September of 1958. The train is approaching Tower 101 and the Hudson River. The Romanesque steeple of St. John's church is a key landmark in Rensselaer. Amtrak's current station, its second in Rensselaer, sits just beyond the second stainless steel car in the train.

(Above) Just about a year later, in July of 1959, we see a very different train roll through the same spot. A brace of Fairbanks-Morse CPA-24-5's lead an all standard consist through the interlocking. The CPA-24-5's were the last order of passenger power placed by the Central with that builder. The opposed piston power was not favorably received on the railroad and the units were re-engined by EMD within three years of delivery. The C-Liner passenger units joined the Erie-builts in service on the upper Harlem out of Chatham for their last summer. They would end up in the deadline at Collinwood Shops within a year of this photograph.

(Below) Gerrit caught this train headed eastbound in Rensselaer in September of 1960. The presence of the rebuilt wood-sided milk reefer suggests that the train is largely express. The torpedo boat GP is one of a series of such units purchased for service on both freights and secondary passenger trains. Business is still holding up, as there is still some local freight in the yard and the B&A main is still double tracked.

(Above) In this early 1950's scene Niagara #6013 rolls right through what will become Amtrak's current Rensselaer station. Within a few more car lengths the engineer will give the engine its head as the tail end of the train clears the wye. A close look at the train shows a string of heavyweight Pullman cars, still a common sight as steam begins to yield center stage on the New York Central.

Englewood was not the only place for races. The southbound LAURENTIAN, now New York Central train #134, is under the control of a classic Hudson. It is passing an E8A-E7B combination as it heads south. The consist includes at least one through coach from the D&H still resplendent in the green and cream colors first introduced for service to the 1939 New York World's Fair. The C&NW Pullman *Mt. Lawrence* may have recently seen the attention of the carman who is watching the events from the shade.

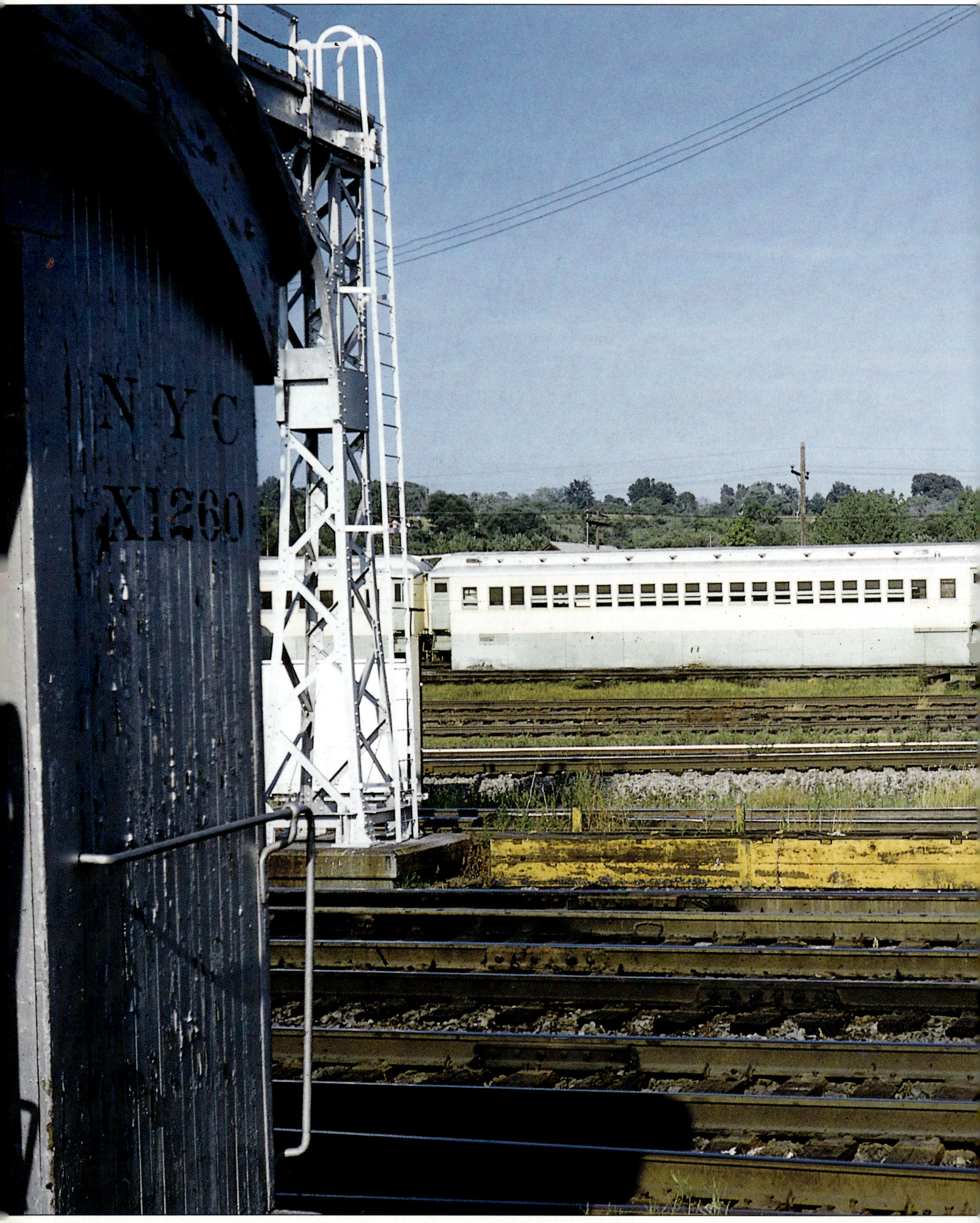
NYC
X1260

(Above) New York Central S-2 #8505 takes a break between shifts in the Rensselaer coach yards. It still carries its original grey scheme, unadorned by any fancy logos. Rensselaer's back doors look almost like a model railroad backdrop. It is likely that these were the homes of a large number of Central employees, as Rensselaer was known as a railroad town.

(Left) Looking across both the Hudson Division and the B&A main into the Rensselaer fueling facility, Gerrit photographed a diesel that looks like it is all trucks. The Baldwin Company produced its baby-faced passenger units in a bid to establish themselves in the growing diesel business. They lost! The units, called "Gravel Gerties" by their crews, were spectacular in their failure even after they were re-engined by EMD and retrucked with Alco-style passenger trucks. Their last service was as a hump set in Selkirk. People always said that Baldwins could really lug at low speed, but the idea of A1A hump engines is a bit unusual to say the least.

(Below) July of 1958, and the local freight yards show much less activity. GP-7's 5756 and 5752 head south in elephant-style formation past the freight house. The train's head end is an interesting mix of refugees from the steam era. Of particular note is the leading express reefer - still in service despite its truss rods. The car's narrow door and its curved fascia strip on the car end suggest that it is a D&H milk car. If so, it has to be one of the last in service.

(Above) June of 1959 sees the Rensselaer local drift passed Tower 100. RS-3 #8224 drills a mix of freight cars in the local yard. Right behind the unit is one of five cabooses rebuilt and painted grey and vermilion for use in "Pacemaker Service". By 1959 the cars had been bumped by the arrival of new steel bay-windowed cars.

(Below) Two years later the yards are empty. The fueling rack is closed and is being ripped out. There is a different RS-3 handling the chores today and the caboose is one of the standard 19000-class cars. Regardless of the change, there is still freight to be worked and the Century green boxcar will be spotted for its customer.

(Above) Gerrit stood on the Broadway overpass to record this view of the fueling area. The 8507 seems to be getting the bulk of attention in this August 1958 photograph. This site fueled and sanded the station jobs, the local roadswitchers and any freight units that ran into West Albany yard. It also administered light running repairs to its assigned units. When it was finally closed, a "temporary" storage tank in the upper level coach yard at the Union Station replaced it.

(Below) In September of 1961, the Rensselaer local spots an RDC-1 for service between runs. It looks like Atlantic-Richfield had control of the fuel contract that month. After this facility was closed, the land was eventually sold off and became the site of a now-closed Price-Chopper supermarket.

(Right) Gerrit sensed a bit of disappointment when he took this photo from the Herrick Street Bridge. The power for this train of conventional coaches was an indication of the importance of the train. The Baldwin "Gravel Gerties" were not a favorite of either the engine crews or the operating department even after their re-engining and replacement trucks. #3203 leads a sister B unit past a string of baggage cars on its way into Albany Union. Although it was not one of his favorite shots, he admits that the subject matter now makes up for his initial disappointment.

(Above) June of 1961 sees well-polished late model E-7A #4025 lead E-8 #4058 on an afternoon arrival into Albany. The train will rattle across the diamonds that take the Boston & Albany out its Post Road branch. After several more turnouts, the train will curve towards the west, cross the Hudson and make a sharp turn back north for its stop at the Albany platforms.

(Below) Same location; this time it is June of 1964. RDC-3 M-487 shows off its clean paint job as it rolls across the B&A. The crossing has been rationalized down to one track. These Beeliners still offered a local service, but they would be move down to the lower end of the division to work out of Croton-Hudson or out of North White Plains on the Harlem Division. RDC-3's featured both baggage and RPO sections and were scarce on the Central.

(Above) A mid-day arrival in March of 1962, an E-7AB combination headed by #4013 leads an interesting westbound consist towards Albany. In addition to the Milwaukee Road baggage car, we can see a Railway Post Office car as well as the usual string of Budd-built coaches.

(Below) April of that year still saw snow on the ground. An unidentified but grimy E-8 leads an unremarkable consist westbound. The train might be any one of a number of New York Central flyers as there is no distinguishing signature item visible in the photo. The only thing we are sure about is the fact that it is not the EMPIRE STATE EXPRESS.

(Right) There was something reassuring and dramatic about steam-heated passenger train. Our leading E-8 shows that the cold of this February day in 1962 has not beaten its ability to generate heat. In the background there is evidence that the B&A crossing was recently reduced to single track. The track gang still has to recover part of the diamond that is still sitting on the ballast beside the lead unit.

(Below) July of 1961 was a good time for rail photography. Gerrit catches a westbound pounding across the B&A diamonds. The second unit is another of the test scheme locomotives painted in black with a low white stripe. Even if the test unit is interesting, it somehow lacks the styling shown when the lightning stripes were clean. The leader today is #4034 and it gives us a nice memory of what used to be.

(Right) Central trains sported a series of distinctive observation cars with a touch of class that ran on a number of special trains. We are looking at the back of a Central train as the Budd Company intended. Even though the observation car lacks a tail sign in this July of 1961 photo, we can guess its identity as train #134, THE LAURENTIAN. One giveaway is the presence of D&H heavyweight coaches in the consist. The other lead is our guess of the approximate time given the angle of the sun.

One morning in June of 1962 saw Gerrit photographing a westbound as it passes the Huyck Felt Mills enroute to Albany Union Station. 4022 leads a parade of mail and express cars which strongly outnumber the two revenue coaches on the back end. There appears to be a working RPO towards the back of the train. The local yard on the left side of the main is in process of change-most likely a permanent change.

Gerrit returned to the Herrick Street Bridge to capture this shot of another westbound taken in July of 1962. Another Rensselaer landmark, the laboratories of pharmaceutical manufacturer Sterling Winthrop seen above the E units, overlooks the Hudson Valley and the NYC. Train #39, THE MOHAWK, still enjoys a hefty consist of summer travelers.

(Above) In a dramatically framed shot, Gerrit captures westbound train #51, the EMPIRE STATE EXPRESS, as it slows passed the now-disused freight house in Rensselaer. The train was scheduled to arrive in Albany at 11:44 a.m. From the smoke of the brakeshoes one can guess that the engineer is slowing for an on-time arrival.

(Below) Under a picture-perfect spring sky in April 1961 Gerrit captures a portrait of a work-a-day team: RS-3 # 8263 and a classic 19000-class caboose. The 8263 had seen more glamorous duties, as it is equipped for passenger service. Given the Central's use of motive power, it may well yet end up hauling passengers in the lower Hudson valley.

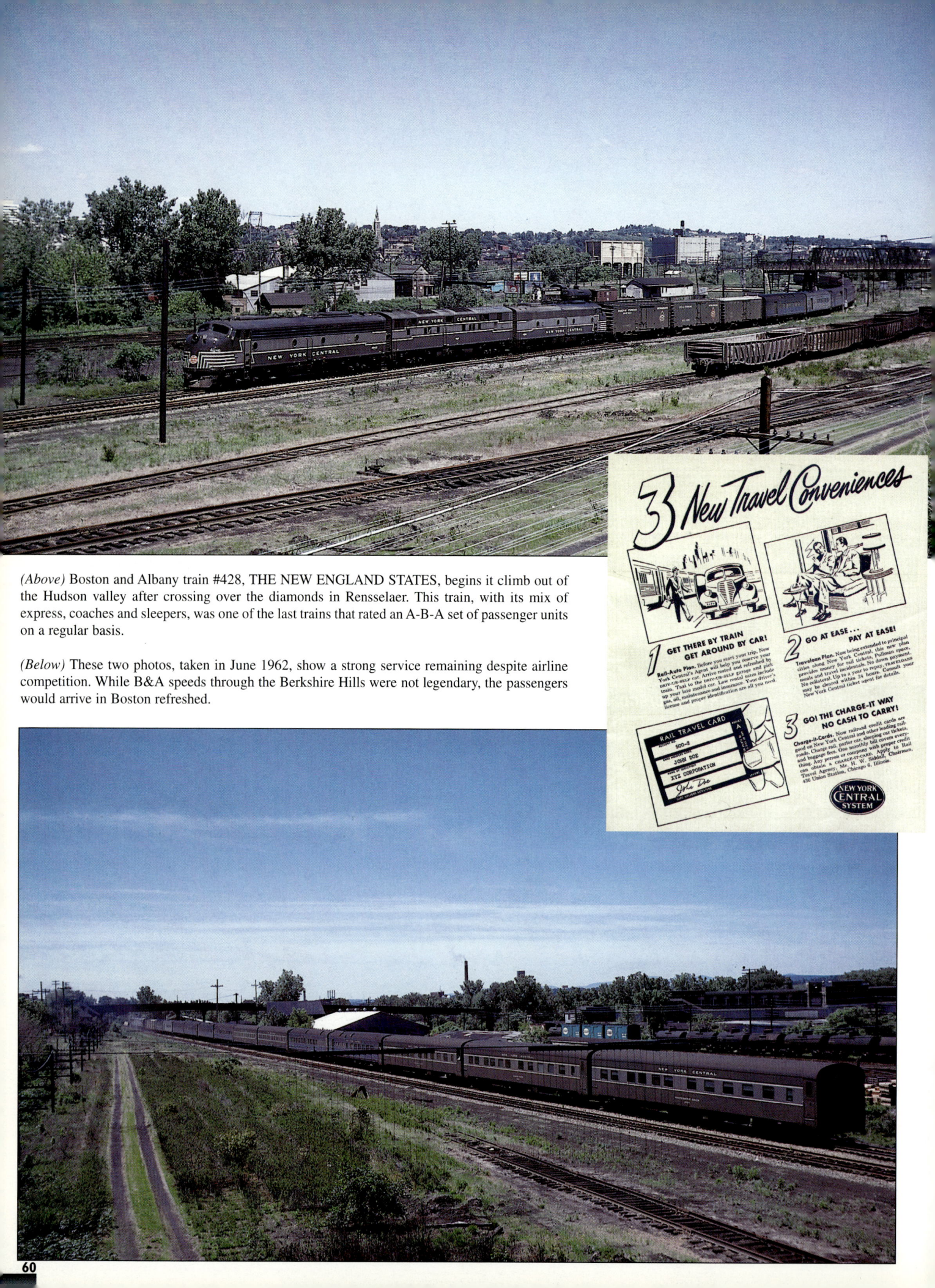

(Above) Boston and Albany train #428, THE NEW ENGLAND STATES, begins it climb out of the Hudson valley after crossing over the diamonds in Rensselaer. This train, with its mix of express, coaches and sleepers, was one of the last trains that rated an A-B-A set of passenger units on a regular basis.

(Below) These two photos, taken in June 1962, show a strong service remaining despite airline competition. While B&A speeds through the Berkshire Hills were not legendary, the passengers would arrive in Boston refreshed.

(Above) Gerrit stepped back a bit from the tracks to catch a potpourri of passenger power in this April 1968 photo. An early Penn Central mail train takes its Flexi-Van train south toward New York showing the ill-fated partnership of this merger for all to see. A Central E-8 leads a Pennsy E-7A, a freshly painted PC E-7A and a sister E-7 past the changing Albany skyline.

(Right) Boston & Albany train #405 rolls downgrade on the Post Road Branch into Rensselaer. The telltales warn anyone riding the tops of the approaching Route 20 Highway Bridge. The snows of this February 1963 scene outline the grade of another railroad company - the Albany Southern. The line is visible just above the RDC. Abandoned in 1929, the Albany Southern operated 3rd rail powered interurbans south to Hudson.

Summer of 1961 brought two more experimental paint schemes into photo range on a southbound train. E-8 4080 leads E-7B #4107 and for once the green scheme looks the better of the two. The interlocking heading towards the Livingston Avenue Bridge has been simplified and they have even cut down on the number of telephone poles.

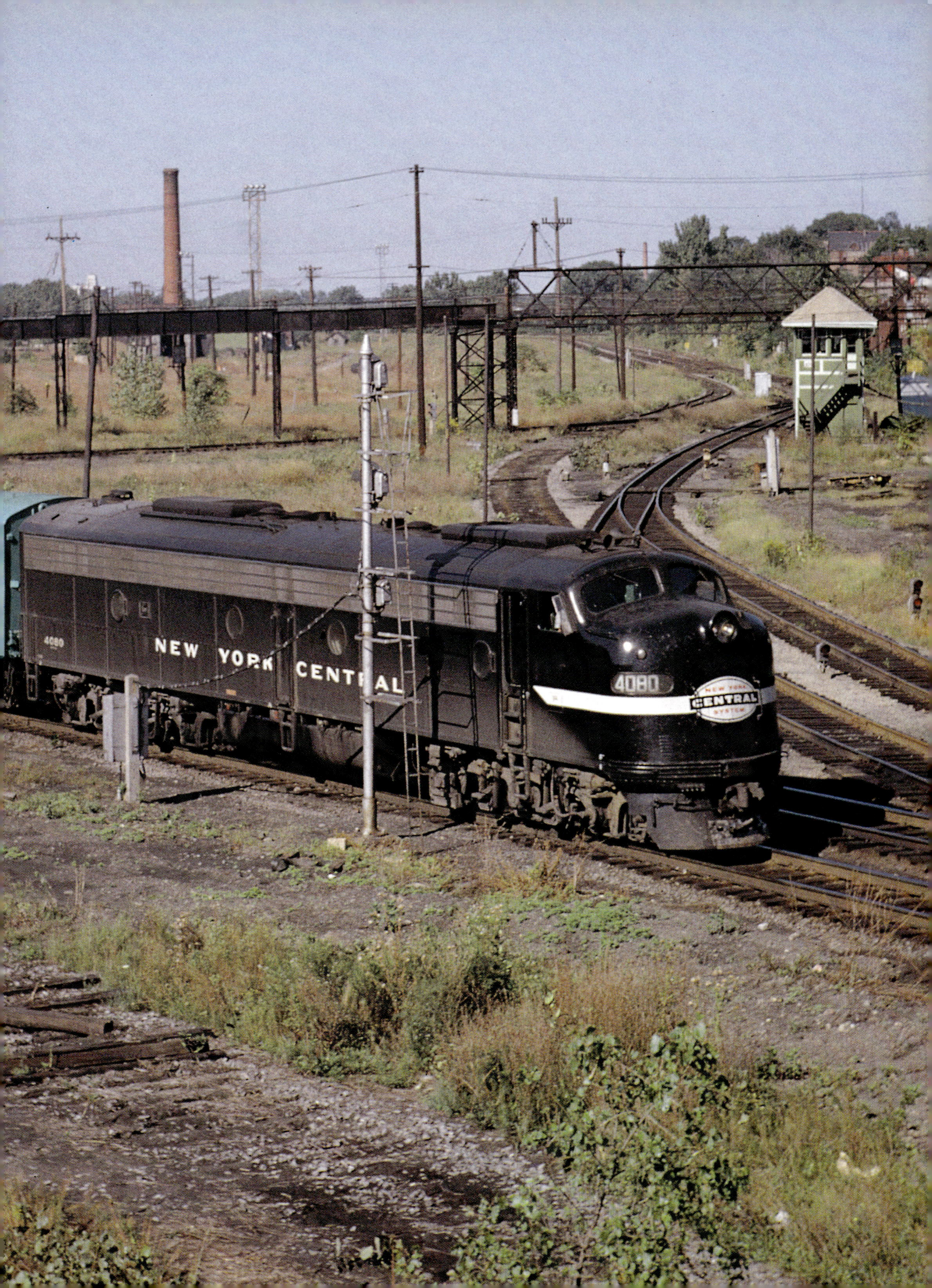

NEW YORK CENTRAL
4080
NEW YORK CENTRAL SYSTEM

(Above) By December of 1963, second generation locomotives began to arrive on the property. GP-20 6111, leading an earlier Geep, has introduced both General Motors turbo-chargers and a new paint scheme to the railroad. Observations of various contemporary photographs suggest that the use of GP-20's on mail or express trains such as this was unusual.

(Below) May 1960 featured this eastbound accelerating off the Maiden Lane Bridge. The passenger yards north of the wye are now empty and will soon be rationalized to reduce operating expenses. Both units, resplendent in classic lightning stripe scheme, represent the New York Central as we like to remember it.

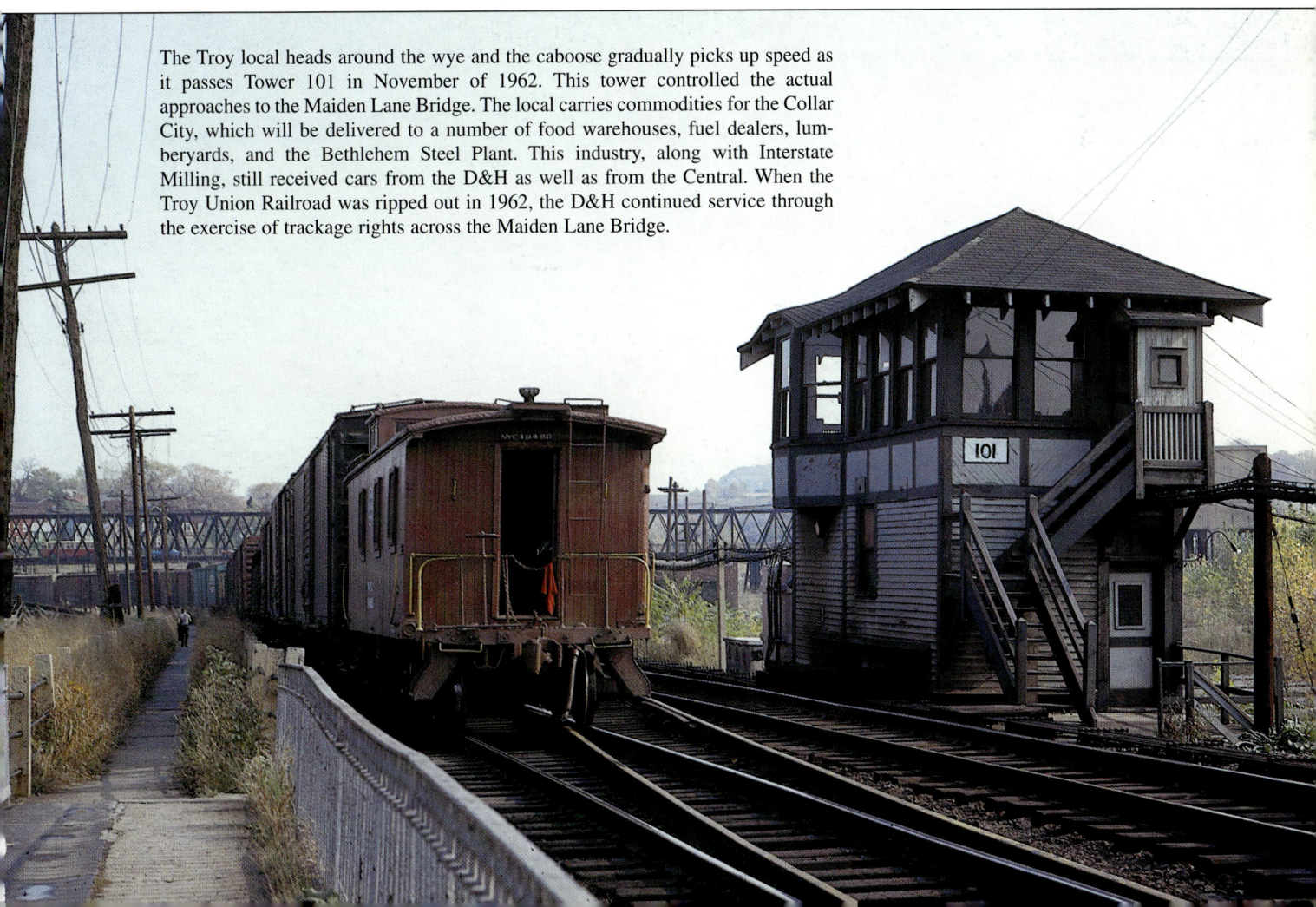

Another express train led by torpedo boat GP-9's #5944 and #5933, both in passenger grey, rolls east under the Broadway overpass. The Central seemed to vary its approach to road switcher paint schemes. This train features grey units while an earlier photo showed a pair in basic black. Even the generalization that Central Geeps lacked dynamic brakes holds true in only a majority of cases.

The Troy local heads around the wye and the caboose gradually picks up speed as it passes Tower 101 in November of 1962. This tower controlled the actual approaches to the Maiden Lane Bridge. The local carries commodities for the Collar City, which will be delivered to a number of food warehouses, fuel dealers, lumberyards, and the Bethlehem Steel Plant. This industry, along with Interstate Milling, still received cars from the D&H as well as from the Central. When the Troy Union Railroad was ripped out in 1962, the D&H continued service through the exercise of trackage rights across the Maiden Lane Bridge.

(Above) In June of 1961, Gerrit captured this shot of an RDC-1 heading away from Union Station. The RDC might well be Train #698, scheduled to depart Albany at 5:15 p.m. and terminating in Poughkeepsie at 6:54 p.m. This was just the kind of local service, which would allow a legislator to make each Assembly or Senate session without having to stay at one of the Albany hostelries.

(Below) Gerrit must have made a favorable impression on the towerman as he was up in the tower again in July in time to capture a shot of a somewhat smaller local freight. It is still headed up by one of the ubiquitous Alco RS-3's. It looks like the remnants of the roundhouse immediately to the right are returning to nature.

(Above) Circus trains were special moves in every sense of the term. In June 1960 the James E. Strates Shows train drops down from the Boston and Maine interchange in Troy after a prior engagement. This was certainly more than a carny show and maintained the tradition of shows under canvas after the bigger outfits moved to auditoriums. The front of the train handled the housekeeping elements of the show needed to erect the tents.

(Below) Once the equipment cars rolled unto the bridge, the cars containing the performers, both animal and human, followed. The show might be heading for a performance in West Albany or might be heading further west into the Mohawk Valley. Since it is rolling west through the station, it is not likely that it will set up anywhere near the downtown area. If the train had been handed off to the D&H for a show in Albany or Menands, it probably would have been interchanged via Green Island.

(Left) Gerrit turned to capture the end of the train as it passed over the Maiden Lane Bridge. The hosting company, as here with the New York Central, provided the locomotives, the crew including caboose and usually a trainmaster to insure that all went well while the show traveled over his piece of the railroad.

Three years later in 1963 Gerrit made his way to the Northern Boulevard viaduct to witness a classic picture of the Albany Gateway - a heavy train fighting its way up Patroon Creek to the summit of the Albany hill. This 1.63% grade was the one obstacle in the Water Level Route. Today's train is an updated version of the Strates Shows train and the Central is hauling it west behind two Alco FA's.

Around this curve about a half-mile ahead is West Albany yard and the summit of the grade. The FA's fight their way upgrade past the start of the Tivoli Hollow branch seen on the right. This is the name given it by locals who watched it wind its way back downgrade. It terminated by Broadway in North Albany, almost touching the D&H.

(Right) Gerrit turned back to the east in time to catch the colorful animal cars rolling past an abandoned coal yard. Bill Middleton caught the EMPIRE STATE EXPRESS at this spot with a classic black and white photo about fifteen years before. The coal dealer had been in business at that time, dispensing both anthracite and soft coal for heating and industrial users in the area. The branch stayed in business until early in the Conrail era, but business was slow by then.

(Right) The tail of the train approaches as Gerrit focused upon the foot of the hill. The Tivoli Hollow branch extended almost all the way to the smoke stacks inching up above the gravel plant in the upper center portion of the photo.

(Below) The noise must have been interesting as one of the station switchers pushes the train up the hill. The speed must not have been too high as the blue haze of the exhaust still hangs close to the switcher. The end of the hill is close, so a trainman has stepped out onto the front steps to make the cut. Several regularly assigned units of both Alco and EMD construction were equipped with mechanical arms to help uncouple on the fly. This pusher ballet began when the line opened in 1844 and sometimes featured as many as two 0-8-0s pushing on the back of the same train. Heaven help the switcher crew which could not make the cut before the summit was reached.

70

(Above) The Albany main line was tied into the upgraded West Shore line in 1927 by a series of major track improvements. Gerrit caught this local coming out of Schenectady to head back to West Albany to tie up. The lines to the left are what are known as the "Carmen Cut-Off". They will cross over the main to the west of this spot enroute to South Schenectady and a junction with the Selkirk branch. The local has come up the main over the Crane Street hill. All of these arrangements were needed to move freight away from the Albany hill. Unfortunately, an off-brand film was used this day and the slide has deteriorated badly.

(Below) Gerrit captured a reminder of the vast amount of traffic once interchanged between the New York Central and the fleets of river steamers across the docks in Albany. The steamship *Peter Stuyvesant* of the Hudson River Day Line repeats a scene that had occurred many times before this. The tracks in the background belong to the D&H and had once played a role in this traffic as well. It may not be a train, but it helps to tell the Albany Gateway story just the same.

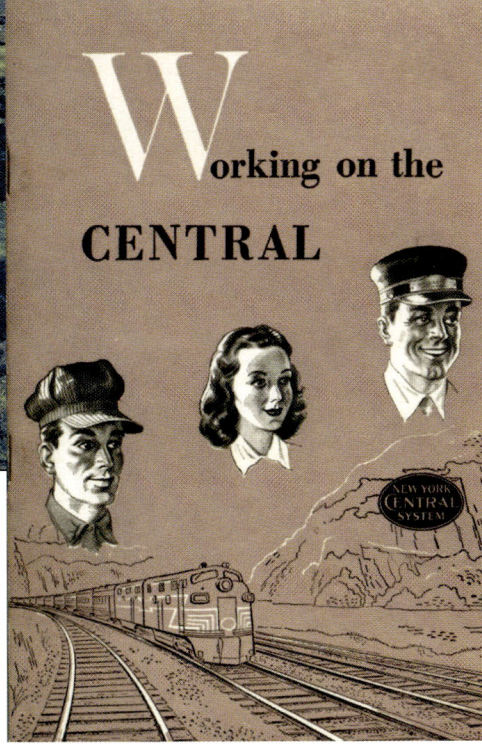

71

(Above) Gerrit ventured outside of the Albany Gateway on occasion, as this October 1961 view on the B&A demonstrates. Chatham served as a terminus for Harlem Division trains to New York; as an interchange with the Rutland Railway; and as a major station on the Boston & Albany. A Beeliner serves as the consist for B&A Train #405 as it slows for a station stop. After much fighting, PC eventually stopped operating 404 and 405, but the station remained until it was finally sold by Conrail to the village.

(Below) By December 1968 many changes were seen here at West Albany. Although the E unit still carries New York Central lettering the Penn Central coach on the tail end marks this westbound as one of PC's EMPIRE SERVICE trains. The West Albany shops that once filled this space are long gone and the pile driver was working on footings for Interstate 90. The West Albany yard still acted as the hub for a number of locals working throughout the Albany area. There are signs of other changes in the neighborhood-note the compressor hoisted up for the weekend.

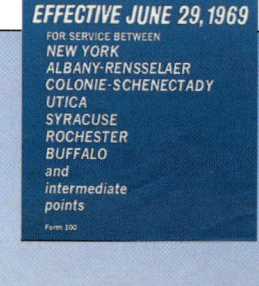

(Above) In November of 1967 the Central accomplished something that it had in its plans since 1959. It moved out of Albany Union Station to a smaller facility in Rensselaer. A B&A mail train stops at the station as it heads unto the Post Road branch towards Boston in order to allow loading of a westbound Empire Service train. With the opening of this station, Penn Central closed the Maiden Lane Bridge. Amtrak later built a bigger structure just south of this one and converted this into offices and a commissary. In 1998 construction will begin on an even bigger Amtrak station which will replace both buildings.

(Left) Schenectady was also replaced with a small economy station in the town of Colonie. In April of 1970 a Penn Central E-8A slows for the Colonie station while a freight heads into West Albany.

By June of 1969, the industrial blight that had settled into the Northeast had also taken root in Amsterdam. Even the Carpet City, as Amsterdam was called after its mills, deep in the Mohawk Valley, had felt the crush of decay. A westbound EMPIRE SERVICE train roll into an Amsterdam station that is long passed its prime. Soon a smaller station on the outskirts of town, too, would also replace it after the onslaught of "Urban Removal".

AMTRAK

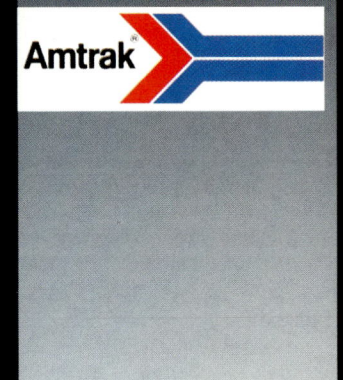

(Above) Eventually Penn Central disappeared and Amtrak evolved as the passenger operator in the Empire Corridor. Amtrak brought more changes with it including the eventual replacement of E units on passenger trains. By November of 1973 the word was out that the E's were going. Gerrit captured #427 in the bloody nose paint scheme arriving from Buffalo. A fair number of passengers are already out on the platform to get their choice of seats for the ride down the Hudson Valley to the Big Apple.

(Right) That same month E-8 #425 brought a small train in from Syracuse. The Central Warehouse rises up out of the river fog providing a reference for our location. The scene will change in the near future as Amtrak builds its Rensselaer Maintenance Facility in this area.

(Right) July of 1974 showed yet more changes in place. Through service to Chicago was restored and New York was funding service to Montreal. New motive power and train sets were appearing and the E units were quickly fading. The Rohr Turboliner on the left has just arrived from its manufacturer in California and has not yet entered service. The SDP-40F and the P30CH (a "brick" and a "pooch" to local fans) are power for THE LAKE SHORE LIMITED. Way in the background sits a D&H PA, waiting for the connecting portion of the ADIRONDACK to arrive from New York.

74

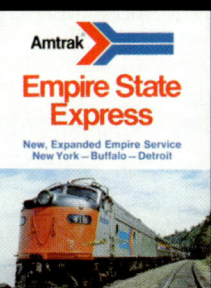

(Above) By September of that year Penn Central #259 was one of the last of the classic E units in service. Albany's skyline has achieved its modern form with the full construction of the South Mall. If you look directly above the unit's front exhaust stack you will look down the alignment of the Maiden Lane Bridge. You can look in vain for any indication of the bridge, Tower 101 or the roundhouse.

(Below) Later that month the changing of the guard was completed when a product of aerospace industry became the latest way to get to Grand Central Terminal. The Turbos introduced a new style of travel and, combined with track improvements funded by the State, provided for three hours service to New York. They started a return to rail travel that has made Rensselaer Amtrak's tenth busiest station in the country.

75

(Left) A bloody nose (formerly PRR) and a striped E combination backs toward the rest of its train as the New York section of THE LAKE SHORE LIMITED gets ready to depart. This ballet of power and cars continued for years as the Boston section was split or united with the train to or from Chicago. This maneuver is planned to end in 1998 when Amtrak upgrades the express portion of both trains. It is planned to operate the sections as two distinct trains in order to simplify train handling in Rensselaer.

(Left) Gerrit captured three old timers in bright colors in this photo. The coach started life on the Erie Railroad before coming to the D&H. The product of Alco just ahead of it was once at home roaring across the Kansas plains or tasting salt spray on a SAN DIEGAN, while the lifting rings on the nose of 447 suggest Pennsy parentage. All three came together in Amtrak service at the platform of a station constructed in what once had been a New York Central yard.

(Below) Running the route and schedule of the old EMPIRE STATE EXPRESS, this photo shows a somewhat begrimed NIAGARA RAINBOW arriving in Rensselaer. The train will brake to a halt in about 200 yards for its station stop. It will then continue west over the Livingston Avenue Bridge and charge the Albany hill. With the closing of Union Station, the Livingston Avenue Bridge was repaired and became the only crossing over the Hudson at Albany. While the city still generates some local freight, the Huyck Felt mill is now closed.

DELAWARE & HUDSON

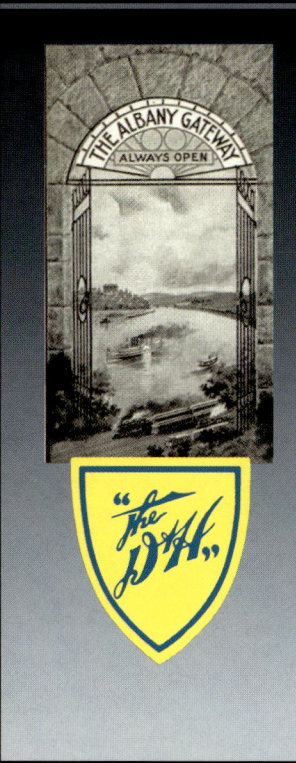

THE ALBANY GATEWAY
ALWAYS OPEN

"the D&H"

(Above) We are looking northwest from the pedestrian walkway of the Maiden Lane Bridge. The coach and RPO are tucked away on one of two storage tracks awaiting departure back to Binghamton. Four baggage cars are set over on the other storage track while two coaches sit on the main line. Albany suffered parking problems, so the vacant space around Union Station was well utilized and filled with a car enthusiast's dream. It's the real thing.

(Below) This ground level view was taken from Maiden Lane in August of 1960. Napierville Junction RS-2 #4051 heads north towards Colonie Shops behind cousin #4016. The Napierville Junction RS-2 retained these colors well into the 1970's when it was finally traded in. It ended up at the Montreal Locomotive Works as the primary component in a rebuilding project destined for Cuba.

(Above) In 1960 train #34, THE LAURENTIAN, still had a sizeable amount of head end traffic. A fleet of REA wagons awaits the packages being unloaded while passengers await the switcher's move of the through cars up to the upper level. There they will be handed over to the New York Central. By the looks of people in the vestibule of the first coach, the baggage cars and diner will be left alone on the track in just a few minutes.

(Below) Two years later, RS-2 #4017, sporting a new livery, prepares to head train #208 south toward Binghamton. The consist is standard for the train in this period: two storage mail cars, a Railway Post Office car and a single coach. The unit shows a moderate amount of weathering, but someone apparently did not pay attention to the fuel overflow.

(Left) In a scene soon to disappear, tardy commuters rush to board the D&H local for Saratoga Springs. The conductor and trainman exchange greetings with passengers who have ridden with them many times before this. Other commuters settle in and begin their review of the evening's *Knickerbocker News*.

(Right) This June 1960 view from platform level shows coach #227 with oil markers attached ready to head north. Although the car is in local service, 227 shows a polished side that reminds readers of the origin of the term "varnish".

(Below) In a timeless ceremony known to railroaders world wide, the crew of this commuter train compare watches, orders and, no doubt, rumors before they assume their assigned positions for departure. #4036 is a boiler-equipped RS-3 as can be seen from the stack on the short hood. The train will leave Albany shortly and its passengers will have completed yet another day of work.

(Above) Mainline freights rarely interrupted the activities of the station. D&H traffic south was traditionally run first towards Mechanicville on trains like AB-4. Cars for Albany left Binghamton on several trains, but BA-3 was the most common. BA-3 was a "hot" train that included long cuts of reefers for the meat and produce markets of the Tri-Cities. It was supplemented by OA-1, an Oneonta train which carried cars from Wilkes-Barre to the Capital District. Both of these trains ran downgrade on the A&S through Kenwood Yard to North Albany. If there were no produce cars, the power would run light from Kenwood to Colonie. Gerrit captured such a power move in this May 1963 photo. This day it rated some of the newest power in the fleet - 5000 class Alcos.

(Below) In October of 1964 the Capital District Railroad Club sponsored one of its fall foliage trips. Club members affix their drumhead to the front platform of #4012, an RS-2 recently upgraded to RS-3 standards. The trip was scheduled to run to Starrucca Viaduct but a derailment rerouted the trip to Binghamton. The train featured open-air gondolas on the rear and a dining car on the head end. This writer can recall both lunch and dinner on the diner, with ice cream smothered in real maple syrup for desert and the sight of Lehigh Valley PA's in Binghamton.

81

(Above) Elimination of local service meant the end of all passenger facilities on the lower level. By August of 1963 the D&H removed excess tracks and had started to shift its mainline tracks closer to the old platforms. The remaining passenger service, consisting of the day and night trains to Montreal, now went directly to a platform on the upper level. Albanians might remember the Hedrick's beer carried by the red Mack truck crossing the tracks. It was operated by one of the last remaining local breweries. The company was owned by the O'Connell family, the mainstay of the Democratic Party machine that controlled Albany politics for over fifty years. It was rumored that every pub owner in Albany complied with the unofficial recommendation to carry Hedrick's Beer- even if they never sold a single keg!

(Below) By 1965 D&H Montreal trains had been arriving and departing from the upper level for over two years. Train #35, THE LAURENTIAN, sits on a February morning with RS-3 4024 ready to go north. This was the late morning routine until the station was relocated to Rensselaer in November 1967.

(Left) Looking every inch like THE railroad engineer, Mr. George N Case prepares to pull the northbound LAURENTIAN out of Albany Union Station. Mr. Case was the senior passenger engineer on the Rensselaer & Saratoga enginemen's roster, having been promoted to engineer in November of 1948. He retired from engine service on 9/14/65, too early to see the arrival of new equipment. His leading unit, rebuilt RS-2 #4009, is also the senior passenger engine on the roster. It outlasted regular D&H passenger service, working locals in the Albany area into the early 1970's. It was sold to the Cooperstown and Charlotte Valley as their #100 and served there until the later part of that decade.

(Below) Three years later and the effects of new management are on display. D&H management, led by President F. C. Dumaine, Jr., decided that the traffic generated by Canada's Expo 67 was worth an investment in cars and locomotives. PA #19 was one of four ex-Santa Fe Alcos that became beloved of enthusiasts. Harsh reality set in shortly after this photo when the D&H realized that northern winters were too tough for single boilers. While the company might not have liked the added expense of running two units it did wonders for film sales.

Two months later, as spring was beginning to arrive, #17 rolls passed Tower B with a mixed consist of ex-D&RGW and ex-EL cars. The 17 was the odd man out of the quartet of Alcos. The Santa Fe had applied new grillwork, forever making it unique amongst a very special fleet of power.

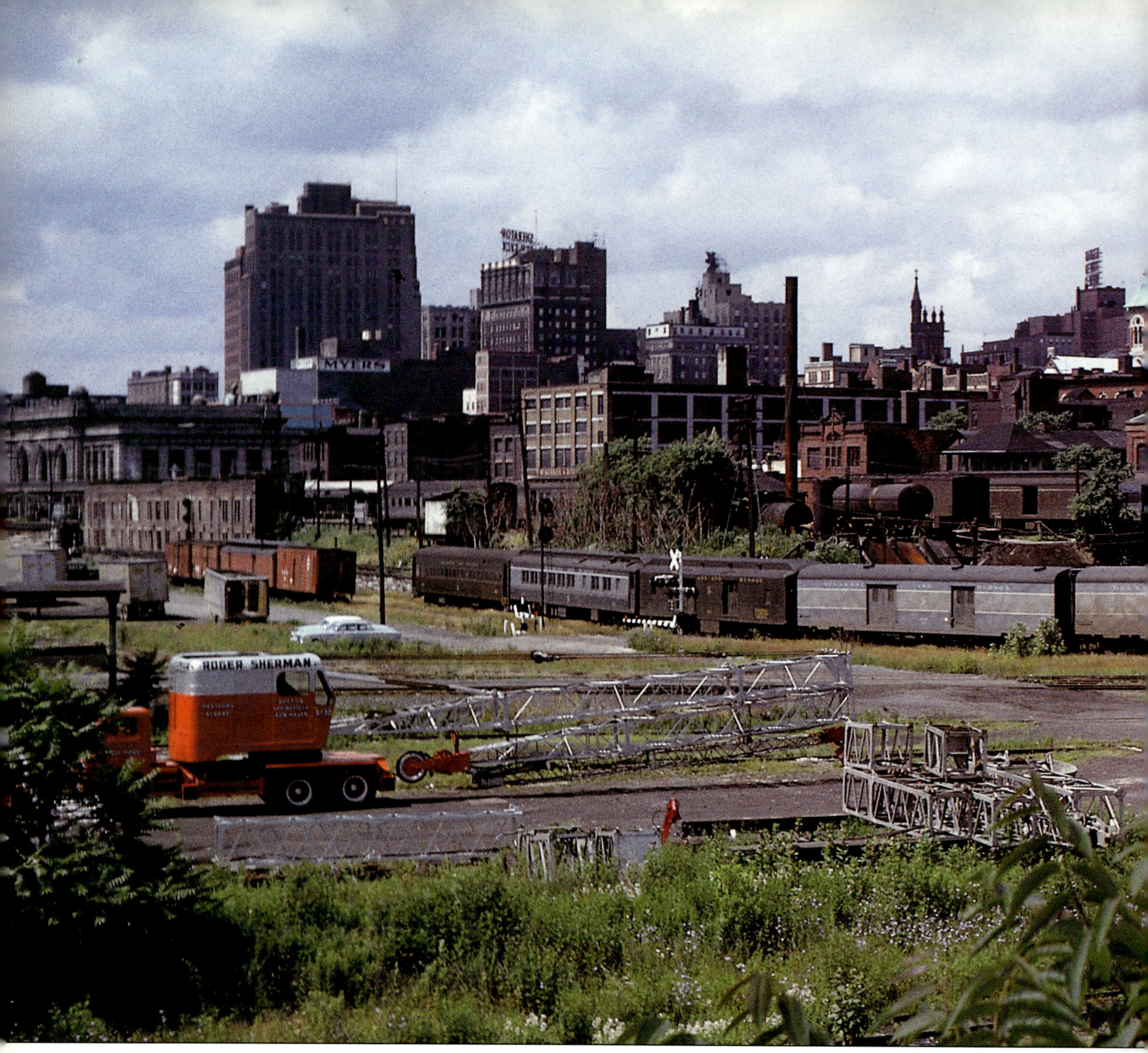
MYERS
ROGER SHERMAN

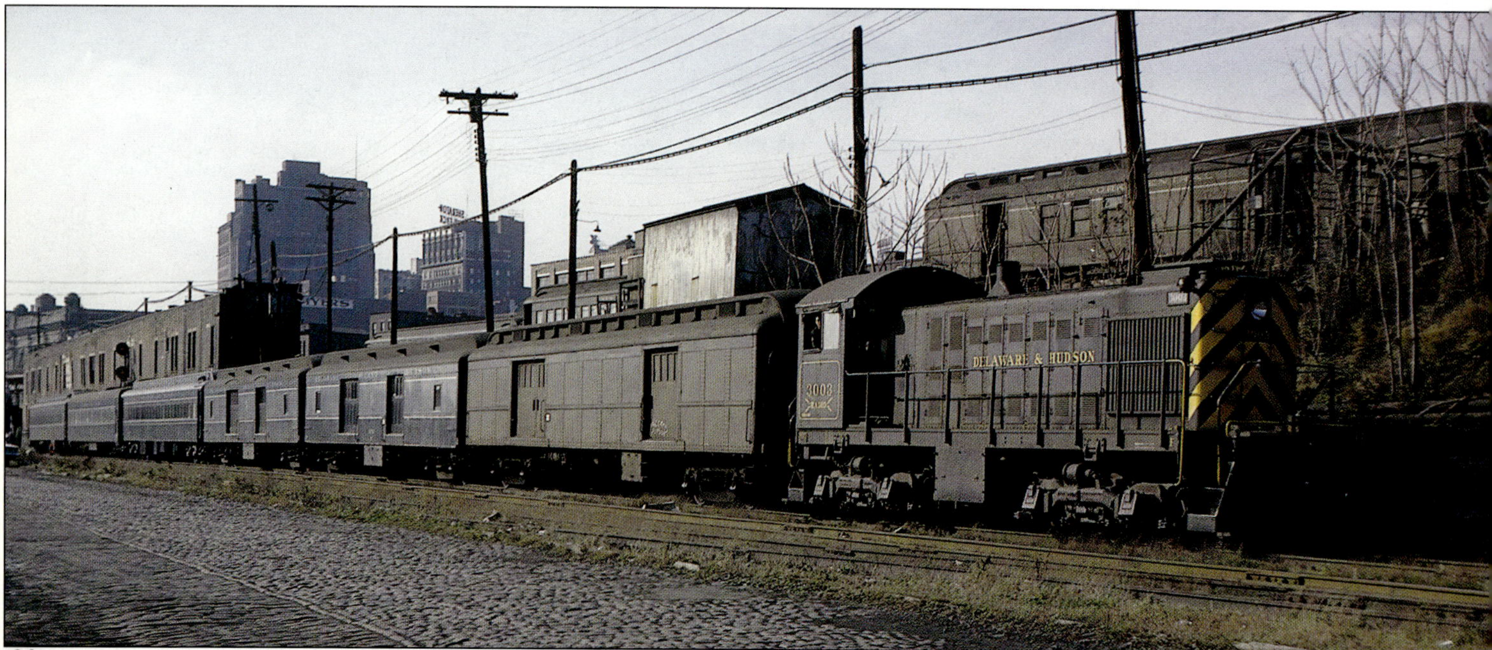
DELAWARE & HUDSON

(Above) We get a different view of Albany as we look west across the north end of the station. A 3000-class switcher shuffles a mixed bag of head end equipment, a diner and coaches on the lower level of the station. The track in the foreground is the Water Street branch of the D&H.

(Left) On a clear December day in 1961 S-2 #3003 shuffles a variety of cars along one of Albany's cobblestone alleys, just north of the lower level station. The D&H used a series of shuttles to move cars between Kenwood Yard, Union Station, North Albany, Menands and Colonie Yard. They moved freight between the yards and industries and moved passenger equipment from the station to the coach servicing facilities in Colonie. The Central's passenger car storage yard can be seen above the switcher.

Mix and match road-switchers bring a train down the ramp from the upper level toward their own mainline. The first two cars are baggage cars purchased by the D&H in 1956 for the magazine trade which was fed by Williams Press in Menands. Millions of issues of *Time*, *Newsweek* and *Life* magazines rolled out for delivery as express car loadings throughout the East and Midwest.

85

(Above) Most model railroaders are forced to accept selectively compressed versions of industries on their railroads - ones that often appear smaller than the cars spotted at them. This June 1963 photo offers a prototype for all of those industries. #12 De Witt Avenue was one of the offices of the Albany Tomato Company, Inc. They proudly advertised their line of business right on the side of the building. Albany Tomato received vegetables from California by the carload and repackaged them for resale locally.

(Below) The New York Central's approaches to the Livingston Avenue Bridge allowed Gerrit this April 1960 view of train #34 crossing the lead to Bull Run yard. Apparently #4008 and #4013 had escaped the addition of the yellow safety stripes normally expected with this paint scheme. Both had been delivered in plain black and may have remained that way until the shops applied the blue and grey.

(Above) Gerrit is standing over Livingston Avenue again as train #35 curves around the main approaching the lower level. It may take a few minutes to cut out Business Car #200 before the switcher can grab the Budd-built parlor observation and the other cars for New York. The switcher will then retrace its steps across Livingston Avenue and push the train up the ramp. The D&H still serviced four different coal dealers off the Water Street branch. Their conveyors can be seen to the left of the mainline.

(Below) Just north of the station, train #34 emerges from behind the old F&M Schaeffer brewery to run through a complex of local yards and industries that stretched up to Broadway in Menands. It looks like a Canadian Pacific express refrigerator is headed home.

Another S-2 #3015 pauses after shuffling some stray Pullman cars about the lower level. This crossing is Clinton Street. It is really more of an alley that cuts under a series of small girder bridges, which carry tracks in the upper coach yard and the station.

(Left) By June of 1959 it was becoming increasingly difficult to find crossings protected by watchmen. A combination of a high level of vehicular traffic and the many switch moves associated with Union Station was reason why this crossing still merited human intervention. The crossing finally closed in 1968 when the whole area was torn up for the construction of Interstate 787.

(Below) #4024 plus another RS-3 approach Livingston Avenue in April of 1960 with Business Car #200, a coach and a baggage car. The sun position suggests a late afternoon move. Since there were no departures scheduled for that time, this is probably a move of cars back to the servicing area in Colonie.

(Right) The D&H would introduce its new motive power to the public in a display on a side track just east of the lower level platform. In June 1961 the newest power was represented by locomotive #5007, a low-nosed 1800 horsepower unit. Called both an RS-11 and a DL-701, it represented the introduction of improved visibility units to the railroad. Modelers will note that the original paint scheme featured a small herald under the gangway steps and a clean blue nose.

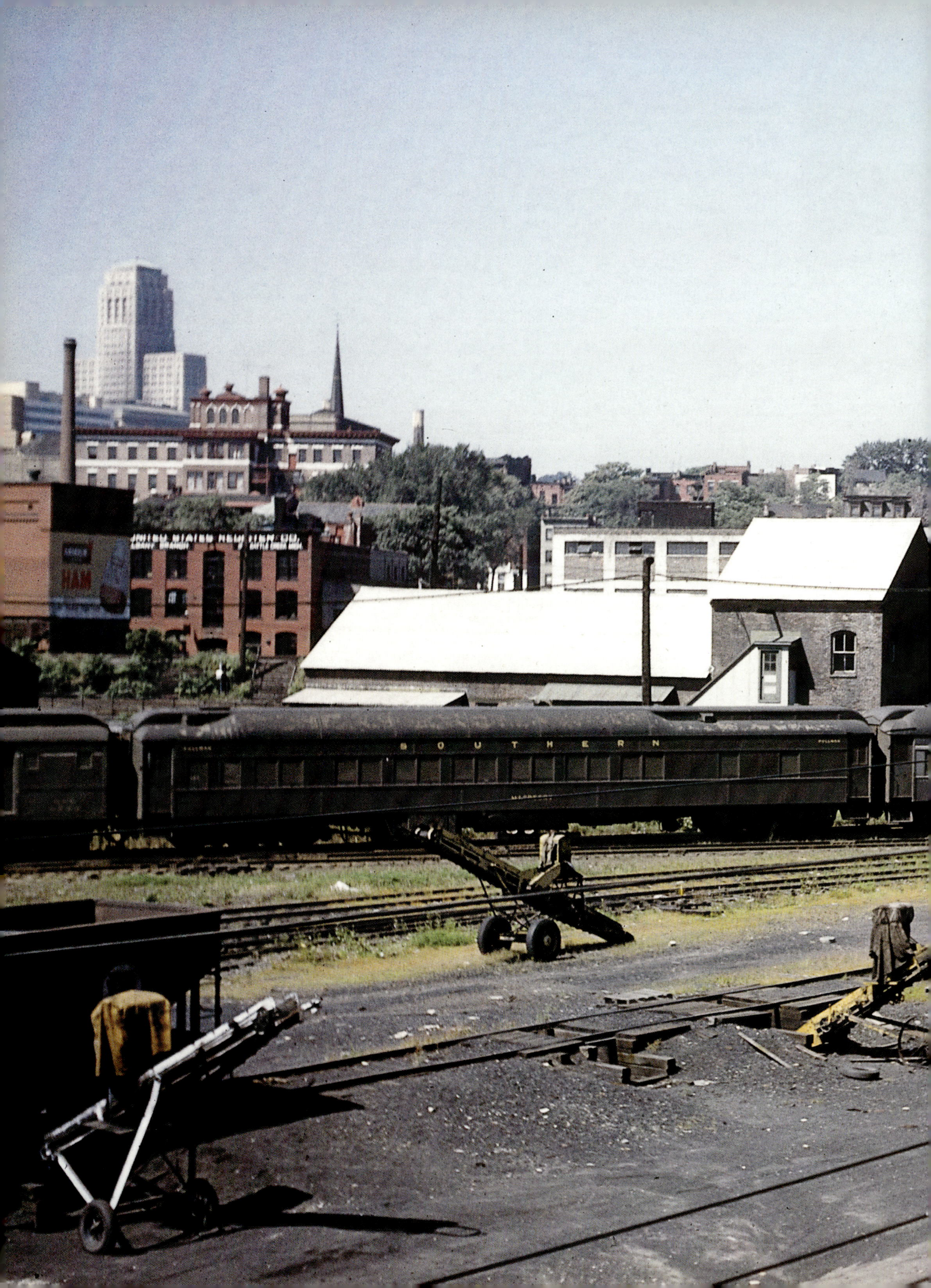
HAM
SOUTHERN

Here is a different view of the Albany skyline. On our left is the A.E. Smith building and on our rights is Arbor Hill. A D&H 3000-class unit shuttles more Pullman cars and a baggage car. The purpose of the Pullmans is somewhat of a mystery. It might be another shuttle to Colonie, but most Pullmans were serviced at a facility at the upper level or in the shops in Rensselaer. We do, however, see that all three of the coal conveyors have been busy.

(Above) We now venture about a half-mile from the station into North Albany, site of one of the feeder yards for local industries. RS-2 #4016 shifts two coaches toward the station while #3026 idles awaiting its shift in the yard. The location is almost impossible to detect now. The highway overpass, Bridge Street, is long gone as is the gas holder in the background. All that remains of that are a Niagara Mohawk parking lot and an EPA hot spot!

(Below) We see Train 34 during that same month. The spotting feature is clearly seen in the form of the NYC parlor-observation. Albany's skyline is clearly seen, with the tower of the D&H Plaza building and the Central Warehouse both against the sky. Most of the freight cars are destined for the Schaeffer brewery. A few others may be headed for McKinney Steel or a paper mill. The baggage cars are probably spotted for Williams Press just north of here in Menands.

(Above) Gerrit visited North Albany and Bridge Street frequently. In September of 1962 he captured two rebuilt RS-2's heading south with the day train from Rouses Point. Like so many other locals, train #18-#4 carried an RPO. The Rouses Point-Albany car was on short time as Postmaster General Sommerfield had decreed its termination. Train #18 started from Rouses Point and did all the local work to back up THE LAURENTIAN. It became Train #4 in Whitehall. Trains #34 and #35 carried through cars, diners and parlor-observations. Trains #18-4 and #3, not scheduled into Canada, carried the US Railway Mail Service in its RPO.

(Above) Another shuttle drifts past the North Albany yard office. #4078 is showing considerable wear and tear as compared with the cupola-less transfer caboose and coaches behind it. Passenger traffic was a loser in 1963 and the company was trying to end service. This had not affected their standards of cleanliness, however.

(Below) By July of that year, blue and grey was the most common scheme for the RS-3's. This northbound shuttle presents a picture of urgency as it moves what appears to be a "hot" car. Despite the appearance, the authors cannot figure out where the REA reefer is headed.

(Left) Train 34 rolls up toward Bridge Street with a heavy consist. The New York World's Fair is still in session- and traffic has seen a mini boom. Three RS-3's lead a goodly train of mixed heritage. The stainless steel cars are from the Central pool. The head end cars are home road cars from the D&H.

(Left) Same location, same month, different train! Two RS-3's working elephant style roll passed a cut of express cars which will soon be loaded with magazines for the reading public. Train #4 still has its RPO, but the train is shrinking in size as other means of transport strip off their share of passengers.

(Below) December's snow put a coat of white on the ground and must have delayed the night train's arrival in Albany. It looks like THE MONTREALER's power set has been grabbed by one of the shuttle crews and is towing a mixed train into North Albany yard. The baggage cars and diner are headed for Colonie, but the freight cars behind the passenger equipment will probably stay in North Albany. One wonders how the crew marked up their time slips for this run.

(Above) By 1965 the 3000-class switchers were reaching the end of their days. The younger S-4's were being MU'ed for transfer jobs. This February day sees a light set consisting of #3042 and 3046 drop passed the North Albany yard office enroute to Kenwood Yard. The decrease in local industry is seen from the emptier tracks - not as busy as in our earlier photos. North Albany would close within three more years but #3042 would outlast all of the other switchers, working the Greenwich and Johnsonville in 1969 to end true switcher operations on the D&H.

(Right) By August of 1966 train #35 was showing the strain. The Public Service Commission had denied at least two train-off petitions by this point. The observation car had been replaced with a conventional parlor and the company was petitioning to remove that service entirely. One bright sign is the block of steel and masonry building up on the horizon. It is a new, modern brewery being constructed by Schaeffer.

In 1967 F. C. "Buck" Dumaine, Jr., was president of the D&H. He was convinced that improvements in service would attract new patronage, especially people seeking a fast but economical route to Montreal and Expo 67. The D&H's own diners were no longer adequate to the task, so he leased temporary replacements. Train #34 rolls through North Albany in October of that year with one such car. The New Haven had extra Pullman-Standard diners that it was happy to lease. This lasted only a short time and photos of them in service have been rare.

(Above) The biggest change brought about by Dumaine was a total re-equipping of the day train, THE LAURENTIAN. Cars originally built for service on the C&O were purchased from the Rio Grande. The motive power arrived from the Santa Fe, and a new era of comfort and style arrived on the route to Montreal. It didn't hurt Kodak sales, either, as this shot along Erie Street shows.

(Below) By March of 1968 the routine was established. If weather was warming, a single PA would haul the baggage car, diner or diner-lounge, coaches and parlor. The parlor was finally lost in 1968 as even the D&H had to face reality. The cars had changed, as Penn Central was reduced to using 10 bedroom 6 roomette cars as day parlors when the supply of traditional cars dried up.

(Below) The D&H line to Green Island hosted a New York Central local, as trackage rights serviced the remnants of the Troy and Schenectady between Green Island and Cohoes. Two or three times a week a Central local, such as this one led by Alco #8504, would run from West Albany to Green Island. During the early 1960s this run occasionally went as far as Niskayuna that included a grade crossing across Interstate 87. It was a challenge when this train flagged itself across the 4-lane highway with the head end brakeman flagging for all he was worth to stop the automobiles.

(Above) Menands is a village within the town of Colonie which adjoins Albany on its north. This business car special with cars #300, #200 and #500 is headed towards Albany in March of 1963. The background of this scene is now marked by the six lanes of Interstate 787. The appearance of the entire active business car fleet on the road was a much sought after subject for Gerrit. While the trip's purpose is unknown, it is likely that President White was out inspecting the property.

(Below) The same location in October of 1967 witnesses the start of the changing of the guard in D&H passenger equipment. The RS-3s are showing their age, as is the second car in the train - the diner. Two recent purchases from the Erie-Lackawanna stand out in their maroon and grey. Four such cars, originally modernized for the ERIE LIMITED in the late 1940s, were acquired to replace D&H heavyweights.

(Below) Several days later Gerrit returned to reshoot the location and train #34. This time he caught one of the leased C&O diners. These cars had originally been assigned to the Pere Marquette and were leased as an interim solution until a decision was made about permanent replacements. Photographs of these cars in service are rare. The only dining car less frequently photographed in service was a Reading WALL STREETER car. The surprise of seeing the car accounts for Gerrit's slight delay in releasing the shutter. Even an old time passenger car devote' could be surprised occasionally.

(Above) A little further north the main north-south highway crossed over the railroad. Broadway (state route 32) was a major route for commerce and had significant railroad customers along its length. Train #34 is crossing under that road in June 1962, still with its NYC parlor-observation. The orange bottle marks the location of the Cott Bottling Company. They made a local beverage which said "If it's Cott, it's Cott to be good!"

(Below) Later that afternoon Gerrit caught a northbound commuter train. It would stop at its first station - Menands - in about half a mile. After that station there were stops scheduled for Colonie, Watervliet, Cohoes, West Waterford, Mechanicville, Ballston Spa and Saratoga Springs. The freshly painted RS-2 lends a colorful introduction to a classic string of Pullman green.

(Below) One month later Gerrit photographed train #34 headed south. The weed grown tracks hide one of the runarounds used in servicing a large warehouse and retail store operated by Montgomery Wards. This complex was an art deco fortress of retailing and had a warehouse behind the store that seemed to swallow boxcars. At Christmas time "Monkey Wards" had one of the largest Lionel layouts around, but the real show was watching a 3000 push cars deep into the warehouse.

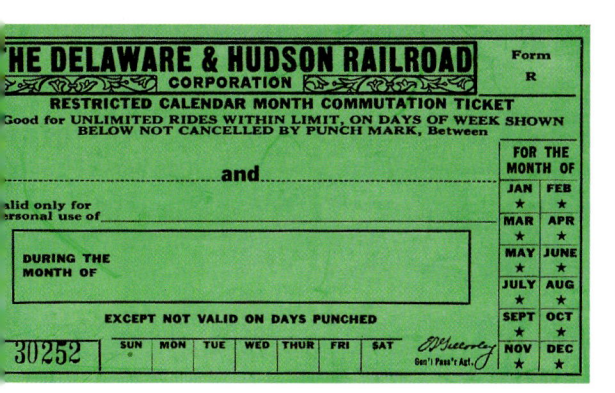

(Above) Elephant style rebuilt RS-2s roll south with a local maid-of-all-work, train #18-4. Note the first car. Its three doors and small windows suggest that this was once a horse car. Perhaps it had delivered its cargo of valuable thoroughbreds to Saratoga Springs for the August race meet and was being returned for another load. It certainly was a more comfortable way of shipping merchandise when compared with the single-sheathed Des Moines & Central Iowa boxcar in the background.

(Below) A train load of commuters heads north in September of 1962, passing some of Menand's bigger industries. The smokestack to the left marks the home of Williams Press. The closer stack belongs to a commercial laundry and uniform service. In the foreground are the tracks of the Breaker Island branch. This led to Menands vegetable and produce markets and was the destination for fleets of refrigerator cars well until the end of the 1950's. Off camera on the right is a White Tower restaurant and, across Broadway, the Montgomery Wards store. The area is what remains of Breaker Island yard. It once serviced a blast furnace opened at the turn of the century but abandoned during the Depression.

(Above) Southbound train #34 rumbles passed the flagstop station in Menands. It is August 1963 and passenger loads are still relatively good, so the accommodations offered by the railroad are still full service-coach, parlor and dining car. Note the signal cabin. It appears that the railroad applied its standard station colors to even its cabins. Ever wonder where Floquil got its "Depot Olive" colors?

(Below) Same place - different train. Commuters hustle home or start their cars for a short drive. The image of the man in the grey flannel suit still holds true in 1962. Ward will soon be home to see what mischief the Beaver has done today. Chances are that most of the passengers live within walking distance of the passenger shelter and will be home shortly without having to deal with traffic congestion. RS-2 #4020 will continue this scene all the way north to Saratoga Springs.

(Above) Gerrit took some time off in July 1962 to catch the morning rush. He stood on the embankment of state highway #378 to catch this southbound. The cars were obtained second-hand from the Boston & Albany in 1956 to replace an earlier fleet of wooden commuter coaches. The location is Menands, just south of the entrance to Albany Rural Cemetery. Opened in the 1870s, Albany Rural is one of the great Victorian cemeteries and home in death to personages such as Chester A. Arthur. It was once served by its own ornate station. Appropriately enough, the D&H named the stop "Cemetery".

(Above) Another June 1962 view of a northbound commuter train rolling passed SG cabin in the town of Colonie. RS-2 #4020 must have been painted recently as the tell-tale sign of fuel spills under the cab side is missing. The ballast along the right of way is still sharply defined and the dispatcher has set up a "high green" for a southbound train.

(Below) The train continues on its way without giving any sign of the number of passengers on board. The daily crowd was shrinking due to improved highway nets and a move of state office workers to a suburban office campus west of downtown Albany. SG cabin was named for South Gate, one of the entrances into the Colonie Shops. The concrete tower off to the left is the original South Gate tower.

101

(Above) Train #34, the southbound LAURENTIAN, accelerates into SG interlocking on its way to Albany. The units are running elephant style; this appears to be a common method of setting up their passenger power. The building in the distance is the old locomotive erecting shop, now converted to be the diesel shop. Off to the left out of the photo are the works of the Allegheny Ludlum Steel Company - a major shipper on the railroad.

(Left) The tail end of Train #35 rumbles across the grade crossing as the train moves towards Watervliet. The New York Central parlor-observation is working one of the last trains using these round-end cars - a fact that may not have been to the Central's pleasure. The car seems to lack its illuminated tail sign. In the distance a local freight hides out on "the third rail" as the D&H still calls its lead into Colonie Yard.

(Right) PA #16 brings Train #35 southbound into the flagstop station at Colonie. #16 is a clue to the changes illustrated here. The grey car in the background is diner #153, finally retired by the arrival of more modern equipment from the Rio Grande. About the only thing not updated in this scene is the platform light. Alas, it too eventually went to scrap.

(Left) As PA#16 begins to accelerate after its stop, Gerrit captured the cause of all this commotion. While only a flagstop opposite the D&H shops, the plywood shelter was hardly bigger than the sigh proclaiming its service area. This is one station sign that escaped any railfan attempts to liberate it. You would need a truck, not a Beetle, to move it!

(Below) Dark clouds provide a background to the last days of D&H passenger service. It is April of 1971. Erie Lackawanna E-8 #821 and a sister bring Train #34 into the final stretch of mainline south of Colonie. The E's augmented the PA's during colder weather and were destined to be a participant in the final drama. Amtrak was coming and with it the end of Delaware and Hudson passenger trains.

Gerrit knew that highway construction offered both new photo opportunities as well as change. He climbed up the bank of a new bridge and grade crossing elimination program for state route 155 to photograph a northbound commuter in July of 1962. In the background sits the large gun shop of the Watervliet Arsenal. The fuel tank sits dead center of the old roundhouse, now gone, and to its right is the diesel shop. Further south are engineering and stores department buildings. The shops were originally constructed in 1915 and modified throughout their lives to meet company requirements. Gerrit captured in one shot what was to be the center of rail activity on the D&H for another twenty years.

(Above) Gerrit returned later that month and ventured out on the still incomplete bridge to photograph a string of commuter cars under the care of RS-2 #4020 heading north. The yard is emptied after the earlier departure of the daily Binghamton-bound freight. While freight car enthusiasts might have enjoyed photographing the variety of car, including Air-Slide cars of flour for Freihofer Baking Company, Gerrit disdained such plebian interests and continued to concentrate on passenger operations.

(Below) Our by-now-old friends head north to Saratoga on another June 1962 day. Gerrit captured the versatility of the all Alco roster as an RS-2 heads up the varnish while an RS-3 shuffles freight in the yard. While some would consider this just routine, Gerrit worked to capture it and especially the passenger runs before it all changed.

(Above) In July of 1962 RS-3 #4069 and a sister pull an unusual train into the North Gate of Colonie Yard. The Boy Scouts of America had their National Jamboree at the Saratoga National Historic Park. Scouts from across the nation went by special train that ended up being hosted by the D&H. Gerrit caught the head end of the train pulling into the yard for watering and servicing at the coach facility before continuing their homeward journey.

(Below) The train was a treasure for Gerrit as it included cars from a variety of railroads and from the Pullman tourist pool. Cars included heavyweights from Pullman, the Louisville and Nashville, the Rio Grande and the Union Pacific. Streamliners came from the Erie Lackawanna (ex DL&W colors as well as the Erie's green), the Santa Fe, and the New York Central among others. For a passenger train fan like Gerrit this was a feast seldom relished in a single serving.

Another view of the Route #155 Highway Bridge sees train #34 coming south in August of 1963. The industry behind the train is Adirondack Steel Casting. Some of their products returned to the D&H as truck frames used on some of the six-axle General Electric freight locomotives rostered by the railroad. The yard job is using the third rail to continue its work while #34 and a light engine occupy both mains.

DELAWARE AND HUDSON

NEW YORK
SARATOGA SPRINGS
ADIRONDACKS
LAKE CHAMPLAIN
FORT TICONDEROGA
PLATTSBURGH
MONTREAL

Eastern Standard Time
Passenger Train Schedules
Corrected to November 1, 1966
EFFECTIVE OCTOBER 30, 1966

Route of the Famous
MONTREAL LIMITED
Between New York and Montreal

(Right) Constructed in November 1949 and upgraded to RS-3 standards, #4023 represents the standard passenger power of the D&H when photographed in October 1964. The unit had recently seen the paint shop and was parked in front of the diesel shop for routine service. Gerrit gives us a good view of the short hood with steam generator and MU equipment readily spotted. Gerrit mentioned a periodic problem faced by the hostlers at Colonie when they sometimes forgot to open the shop doors before moving the units. We wonder if they remembered to move that ladder as well.

(Right) Gerrit bent his rules regarding freight equipment in order to grab a portrait of a pair of outsiders in this February 1975 photo. Baldwin RF-16A's #1216 and #1205 pose in front of the shops in full warbonnet scheme. They became very familiar with the shops as their unique prime movers and electrical systems made them the hanger queens of the Sterzing era. Originally built for the NYC, they had been obtained from the Monongahela Railway for their weight in scrap.

After the birth of Amtrak, the D&H continued to use the PA's for business trains and other special moves. In June of 1971, Gerrit joined a number of other fans to watch as units #18 and #16 couple up to the Café Car and prepare to start another trip. The event is newsworthy as Jim Shaughnessy joins in the photography. The SP high-cube auto car in the background is stored on one of the now-excess coach tracks. It will be loaded at the Ford radiator plant in Green Island and routed back toward Detroit.

(Above) Among D&H fans, color photos of Car #400 are rare. It was donated to the Museum of Transportation at Kirkwood, Missouri, in 1963. This was long before most fans became interested in such items. Gerrit caught it at Colonie in the late afternoon sun. The light helps to show the early steel sheathing. This Pullman product of 1914 was clad in simulated wood sheathing in hopes of decreasing the fears of electrocution voiced by some of the more conservative members of the public.

(Below) A little exhaust drifts clear of the stack as the RS-3 rumbles north over the 20th street crossing in Watervliet. The station is closed and up for sale. No buyer will be found so the station is now an open lot next to a diner. Gerrit caught this departure during June of 1962. The service was in its last days and the stations along the route were no longer of use. Flag stops and shelters would soon replace them.

In July of the following year Gerrit climbed to the top of the embankment carrying the Troy and Schenectady over the D&H. Train #35 has just passed headed southbound. The junction with the line to Green Island and the old Rensselaer and Saratoga is seen above the train. To the right is the complex of Behr Manning, a major maker of sandpaper and other abrasives. Ties stuck between the rails of the old southbound main enforce an out of service order. The track will soon be torn out as part of a rationalization program.

(Right) Years earlier Northern #307 interrupts a summer morning's play for at least one young man. The 4-8-4 is moving through Green Island's yard tracks after crossing the Hudson River from Troy. A number of D&H passenger trains avoided Albany Union Station and were routed through the Collar City during the summer months. #307 will shortly join the main line and continue north. Sun angles made this a tough shot, but Gerrit trusted his Leica to capture this now rare shot.

(Below) In the late 1950s the State of New York funded a major line relocation in order to move the railroad out of the middle of downtown Saratoga Springs. One part of that project is this rather utilitarian station. Late September light in 1962 illuminates a standard consist ending its run. At time of publication this same station serves four daily Amtrak trains.

109

(Left) In April of 1968 the Mohawk and Hudson Chapter of the NRHS operated an excursion on the D&H's day train to Fort Edward. Gerrit delayed reboarding the southbound long enough to catch this portrait. It was a fan trip on a regularly scheduled train, but the crew was friendly and the ride fun. A few of the fans were even allowed a visit in the cab of the PA. Recognize anyone you know in this photo?

(Below) Three years later and the fans are photographing the train in a different mood. At the end of April 1971 the National Railroad Passenger Corporation, or Amtrak, took over inter-city passenger operations. There was no provision in the initial system for service to Montreal. A pair of EL E-8's provided the power on the southbound as it pulls into the station at Fort Edward.

(Right) Late in 1967 New York Central moved its passenger operations to a new, simpler station in Rensselaer. The D&H relocated as well. Gerrit caught this portrait during April of 1970. This daily show had another full year to run before the curtain lowered for the last time.

(Right) Erie Lackawanna E-8A #820 and a sister have arrived in Rensselaer and are preparing to hand their through cars from Montreal over to Penn Central for transit to Grand Central Terminal. It may be April of 1971 but the car knockers are still wearing the kinds of clothes that might have been associated with this same spot a generation earlier.

(Below) Not much of a train today, which may help to explain its coming fate. Two EL E-8A's will surrender the coach and then reverse to return for service at Colonie Shops. This cycle had only a few days left in which to run.

The weather is warming and traffic is a little better on this day in April of 1971. A single unit propels five cars on the last few yards of its trip. Oddly enough, conventional rail traffic had a better chance of survival than that tube in the foreground. It was an experiment conducted by Rensselaer Polytechnic Institute in which a scale model vehicle was propelled through the tube by a gas-powered lawn mower motor. It was an early and unsuccessful attempt at an air cushion vehicle.

(Left) Sometimes the last month of service produced bigger trains than normal. Blue-grey Alco exhaust drifts down over the train as the pair of PA's pull out for a run up Albany hill for their own tracks in Schenectady. All 4,000 horses will be needed to maintain track speed while going up that 1.63% grade.

(Below) To everyone's delight the State of New York performed a miracle in 1974 when it not only funded Montreal service but also actually reprieved the PA's from death. Gerrit captured a special moment from the Broadway Bridge that August as another photographer prepares to capture a portrait of the returned units. The photographer again is Jim Shaughnessy. The domes were an added touch, leased from CP Rail to highlight the beauty of the Champlain and Hudson valleys.

The problem of powering the new trains while rebuilding the PA's was addressed through the use of stand-in power. This was simplified when the D&H traded two freight RS-3's to the B&M in exchange for two different models. Ex-B&M #1508 leads this pair in Rensselaer on a day in November of 1974. The angled number boards and the body vents are the recognition features of this phase III unit.

112

(Right) #17 leads a sister passed the Central Warehouse on its start up Albany hill. Trains were once again routed over the Livingston Avenue Bridge due to the construction of Interstate 787 in the background. This highway net covered the tracks of Union Station, destroyed the Maiden Lane Bridge and obliterated Bull Run Yard. In the process, I-787 isolated Albany from its river front.

(Below) The high school peeking out in back of #18 gives away our location in Rensselaer. Our train awaits its New York connection. Once here, the train will head for Schenectady and the seats in the dome car will fill quickly.

In April of 1971, Gerrit captured a pair of PA's westbound for Schenectady. The station is Colonie-Schenectady, opened in 1968 when Penn Central closed service to downtown Schenectady. While the building stands at time of publication, one could easily mistake it for a car wash. But then, some of us made that mistake back in 1968!

(Right) Our tour of D&H operations in the Albany Gateway now turns south. Standing just south of the Maiden Lane Bridge, in March of 1960, Gerrit captured a black and yellow RS-3 shunting a coach and a diner passed the Plaza Building. The small tower and attached building to the left of the main tower was actually added to the complex after its original construction. The publisher of the *Albany Journal* newspaper built the building at the south end of the Plaza.

(Below) South of the Plaza Building along Broadway was a team track complex built in about 1915 when the D&H cleaned up this stretch of waterfront. Southbound train #208 begins its run to Binghamton. The variety of freight cars testifies to the number of different businesses still served from these tracks.

(Left) We see a similar scene in September of 1959. Train #208 is in its usual formation of 2 or more baggage cars, an RPO and a single coach. We also get the idea that the railroad could still compete on long distance moving, as the Vogel truck belonged to one of the major moving companies in the Albany area.

115

(Above) In September of 1962 Gerrit again caught Train #205 on its last mile before arriving in Union Station. The abandoned tracks in the foreground once served interchange traffic with some of the river steamship companies that served Albany. The ramp on the left takes automobile traffic up to the Dunn Memorial Bridge and Rensselaer. The overhead crane from the team track still exists, as it was relocated to a new location in North Albany when the state buried all of this under highways.

(Below) The same train is seen earlier in that same year - in June. New public housing is seen in the background, as are some of the remaining light industries that once filled this area. A number of industrial tracks spin off from the main, giving an idea of the traffic that once fed into Kenwood Yard.

CORRECTED TO JANUARY 9, 1944

Delaware and Hudson Time Tables

Susquehanna Division
SCHEDULE OF TRAINS BETWEEN
ALBANY ALTAMONT
COBLESKILL
ONEONTA SIDNEY
BINGHAMTON

R. T. GILLOOLEY, General Passenger Agent
ALBANY 1, N. Y.

(Above) By January of 1963 Train #205 and its counterpart #208 were on their last legs. #205 moves passed KN tower, the junction between the Albany and Susquehanna and the West Shore. Kenwood Yard, located to the left of this picture, served local industries including export grain at a GLF elevator in the port, a milling operation, several oil storage facilities, a molasses dealer, scrap yards and a steel fabricator. While much of the scene is now covered with Interstate the neighborhood store remains in service under different management.

(Above) Southbound Train #208 pauses at KN tower. The RS-2 leads a routine consist of express cars, RPO and coach for the run over the Susquehanna Division to Binghamton. This July 1962 scene depicts an average day at Kenwood. The yard's safety statistics are displayed for all to see on the large cast iron sign facing the yard tracks. Things must be going fairly well, as an employee has parked a classy Buick convertible adjacent to the tower. It looks like the day was so nice that he probably rode to his second shift job with the top down. The streamline baggage cars outlasted the service by only a few years. Loss of these trains combined with changes in magazine publishing practices put the cars on the second hand market in 1965. They survived their sale to other carriers, as this author saw one in a GM&O train departing Union Station in Chicago in October of 1969. It still sported its two-tone grey paint even though it was lettered for the GM&O.

(Right) Late one November afternoon in 1962 Gerrit ventured out into the village of Elsmere while visiting his sister to a location just off Rockefeller Road. Looking east toward Kenwood Yard and the Hudson Valley, he caught the Binghamton train stretched out on the line. This grade was always a challenge for the D&H and was a primary reason why outbound freights were routed north and then west via Mechanicville.

(Above) Train #208 heads downgrade towards the Port of Albany on another November 1962 day. The train's reason for existence as far as the railroad was concerned was the revenue from the Railway Post Office. The train usually had one working postal car and a storage car. On a busy day there might be a second storage car. Within two more months NRHS members from Binghamton were to ride a "funeral train" on its last day, their protests were ineffective and resulted in only an interesting photo in the evening paper.

(Right) January 1944 Susquehanna Division Timetable.

(Below) Snow has highlighted the ground as train #205 passes Rockefeller Road eastbound in another view. The starkness of the ground shows little indication that this scene is within three miles of the city limits of the capital city. The steel of the Delaware Avenue Bridge overshadows the dairy barns in the background. By 1962 Albany had begun its move into the suburbs and the future of the dairy farm was about as secure as the future of #205. Still, there is an almost Christmas card sense to this scene.

(Above) Train #208 heads back to Binghamton in this November 1962 photograph. Gerrit was able to catch the final fading colors of autumn in the trees as the RS-3 accelerates. The scene is typical of the Albany main - single track through small communities that were gradually changing from rural to suburban. No local service remained on this line during that last November of service. The train will make its first real stop in Delanson. All other stations between Albany and there were treated as flagstops. The flanger sign in the foreground is only decorative now. Within a few weeks it may well be needed to warn plow operators of the grade crossing just ahead.

(Below) The train skirts a ridge top in January 1963. The barren scenery is appropriate for a snow-less winter. It is a reflection of the bleak future of the train and, at least for now, the line itself. The D&H gradually rerouted all but local traffic off the old A&S line. CP Rail still only runs an occasional local to the industrial park in Voorheesville and the line beyond there to Altamont and Delanson is embargoed. Perhaps its future will change to the good as the railroads of the Northeast move into the post-Conrail era.

MISCELLANEOUS & EQUIPMENT

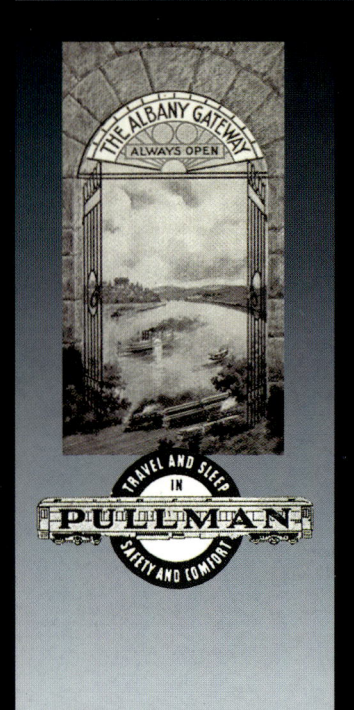

(Above) Vegetation control has always been a challenge. If not accomplished, weeds choke the ballast and prevent good drainage. This causes maintenance problems. Burning was one method, and this New York Central weed burner gives a display of this smoky technique in the Sand Lot in Rensselaer during September of 1959.

(Above) Chemical Warfare is used too. In July 1960 the New York Central sprayed the wye leading to the Maiden Lane Bridge. There was a different standard regarding protection of the spraying crew back then. One wonders exactly what type of herbicide was being sprayed from the tank cars and how much of it really got to the right of way.

(Left) The D&H used weed control contractors as well. The Nalco train sits on the Maiden Lane crossing on the lower level of Union Station in June 1960. It was probably spotted there to assist the crew in making adjustments to its load. Once again we wonder just what was in the barrel.

120

(*Above*) Well into the 1950's one of the largest hotel operators in the United States was the Pullman Company. Despite anti-trust actions taken in 1946 to split the car building business from the car operating business, the name remained permanently associated with sleeping cars. One such car, *Lake Catherine,* sits in the Sand Lot awaiting its call to serve as part of the Great Steel Fleet.

(*Below*) While the paint schemes varied, conservative green was a trademark of the sleepers. This Southern Railway-owned car sits alongside a red Pennsy car in the upper level yard. By this time the heavyweights had been placed in reserve and were usually seen in seasonal or special service.

In July 1958 Gerrit photographed an older New York Central heavyweight converted to serve a new purpose. Diesel Instruction Car #X8012 provided a portable classroom to assist engine and maintenance crews make the conversion from steam to diesel. It is seen ready for service in the Rensselaer coach yard. The blind end vestibule and the small windows suggest that we are looking at the kitchen side of a converted diner.

(Above) Passenger cars carried lead-acid batteries to provide lighting for passengers. Batteries need recharging and cleaning, which means the railroad had to move them to centralized shops to do this safely and efficiently. Battery Car #X24010, shown here in Rensselaer, was one of the cars to do the job. Corrosion was not a problem for a wood-bodied car.

(Below) Railroads are a dangerous business. One moment of inattention could lead to a disaster, so the fight for safety awareness is ongoing. In April of 1962 Gerrit caught New York Central #X23177 in fresh safety green and white paint. This mobile classroom was moved from yard to yard to preach the safety credo.

(Left) In April of 1962 this car came south on D&H train #34. Gerrit's keen eye for passenger cars recognized the difference in it immediately. The three doors, small windows and end loading doors show that this had originally been built to transport horses. While the D&H had hosted many such cars before this, the April date of the photo is out of season for the annual meet at Saratoga's famed flat track.

(Above) New York Central Rules Examination Car #X23415 was a familiar sight to Central employees. All operating employees had to pass an examination of their knowledge of the Book of Rules at time of employment and periodically after that. The rules car moved about over the division conducting its classes and examinations as required. This heavily modified coach served that function until replaced.

(Below) There was something stylish in the Central's two-tone grey styling and Gerrit's photograph of *Otsego Lake*, a six-bedroom buffet car, almost has an advertising quality about it. The lines of the Mercury seem to compliment the understated elegance of the sleeper. Unfortunately the changes in passenger tastes resulted in sister cars ending up in commuter or even maintenance of way service before meeting their ultimate end as scrap.

Where a version of the Central's greys graced D&H passenger equipment for many years, the railroad had gloried in its own unique mix of paints in the 1940's. Coach #222 is seen on the lower level of the station shining in its own version of the paints introduced with the arrival of the first streamliners for service to the 1939 World's Fair. The green and cream was offset with tangerine striping, distinguishing D&H cars from any others. These colors graced a variety of car types, eventually including at least one wood bodied combination car used on the Lake George trains.

The days were numbered for car #35222 when it was photographed at the Colonie coach yard in July of 1963. The car was originally constructed as a coach by Wasson in 1893 and had been upgraded in 1927 and renumbered #653. The car was renumbered into the maintenance of way series in 1952 and ended its service as the rules car shortly after the photo was taken. A steel commuter car freed from revenue service when the locals to Saratoga were cancelled eventually replaced it.

(Left) Business cars were always treated as the flagship of the passenger car fleet. Entrance was subtituly barred with the gilded notice of "Official" on the door. Car #300 came to the D&H with W. H. White from the New York Central and would go with him to the Erie Lackawanna. The car served until the end of that railroad and survives in preservation.

(Below) Car #500 had served the D&H since its construction by the Pullman Company in 1917. In March of 1967 it was repainted into a unique scheme of berry red accented by gold stripes. No one seems to know why these colors were selected, but the combination is generally credited with being the snappiest scheme used on the office cars. #500 was painted into the Champlain blue scheme within a few years and served in those colors until sold to Mexico in 1978. Its fate since then is unknown.

THE TROY BRANCH AND B&M

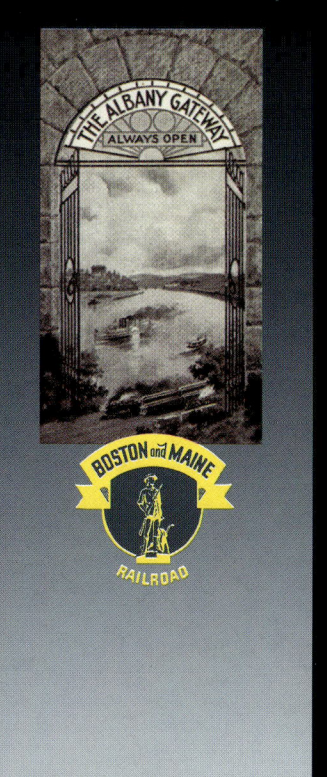

(Above) New York Central Pacific #4388, a K3q class built by Brooks in 1923, begins to accelerate southbound out of Troy's Union Station. Gerrit did not spend much time in Troy, which is not surprising considering the big show in Albany and the declining passenger traffic in Troy. B&M trains connected across the platform with the Central and even that traffic was changing quickly. The B&M was an early advocate of the Budd car, while D&H operations were largely seasonal and the Rutland ended its passenger service in 1953. Steam was quickly disappearing-almost matching the speed which this Pacific's 79 inch drivers would reach enroute to Albany. *(Jeff English Collection)*

(Left) Union Station stretched out a full city block, so Gerrit caught a rather frequent event involving unusual equipment. This view from early 1950 shows Troy's early version of gridlock as a train makes a station stop. It effectively cut off part of the city from downtown. The train includes Pullman cars - which makes it unusual for this late date in Troy. Gerrit stood opposite of the Railroad YMCA, just visible on the right, and captured the flavor of this section of the downtown. It is completely gone now.
(Jeff English Collection)

(Left) He moved up the Approach to include a bit more of Troy's downtown in this view. The Approach was a formal entryway between downtown Troy and the academia of Rensselaer Poly-technic Institute, situated on the hillside above the city. The stairway featured a series of classic columns, two of which frame the photo. Unfortunately age and disuse allowed the Approach to decay until it resembled a classical ruin more than a functioning gateway. The station was torn down in 1958 and only a keen eye can now discern its old location on Sixth Avenue. *(Jeff English Collection)*

125

(Above) The B&M maintained a small freight yard and roundhouse at the foot of Middleburgh Street in North Troy. Several stalls of the roundhouse were retained for temporary equipment storage after dieselization. The longest just fit an E-7 and the turntable was able to turn the power after each run from Boston. E-7A #3815 is lined up to fit into the end stall in this photo taken in the early 1950's. *(Jim Odell Collection)*

(Left) A roundhouse must provide for both locomotive servicing and crew facilities. The B&M had economized in its physical plant in Troy by using old railway cars "temporarily" placed by the roundhouse. Gerrit's interest in passenger equipment made photography of the crew quarters mandatory. The open platform coach may have had its underframe sheltered from the wind but a check of the books will find the car still in company service. No sense in adding to the property tax bill if needed. The same stands for the supply car next to it. *(Jim Odell Collection)*

(Left) In addition to the freight yard, the B&M dedicated several tracks to passenger car storage. Coach #4596 shows some road grime while laying over in Troy. Built by Osgood-Bradley, the car was one of the series nicknamed "American Flyer" after the models manufactured by the toy train maker of the same name. Conventional equipment was giving way to Budd cars, so Gerrit risked an intrusion into the yards for a portrait. He did not seem to bother the canine in the photo. Rover seems more intent on getting across the yard than in protecting the lead to Collins Lumber from some silly railfan. *(Jim Odell Collection)*

(Left) Gerrit caught early morning preparations in this view from the Rensselaer Street overpass. We are looking north towards Middleburg Street. An E-7 has moved out away from the lead and is crossing the street under the careful eye of a watchman high in his crossing tower. The unit will follow the passenger cars being selected by the red and yellow switcher south to Union Station. There all will be put together for another eastbound bound for Johnsonville, Greenfield and Boston. Gerrit captured some other items of interest in this view. Included in it are two baggage cars converted from troop sleepers, a B&M reefer and the open space that once was the coach storage area.

(Jim Odell Collection)

RUTLAND IN RENSSELAER

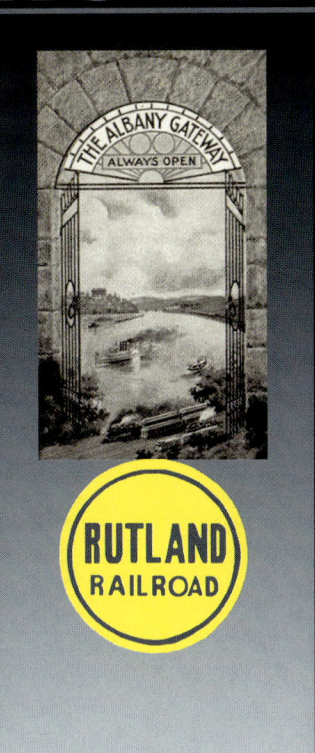

RC-4 passes an inbound RDC as it reaches the switch leading to the Post Road branch of the B&A. The train required specially qualified crews and locomotives fitted with Automatic Train Control in order to make its passage to Chatham. No work was performed after leaving North Bennington and the train reversed its direction once it finished its work in Chatham. *(Jeff English Collection)*

Rutland history is displayed as the green and yellow caboose rattles passed Tower 100. During the early part of the Century the New York Central had exercised control of its Green Mountain relative. This control was manifested in similarities of design in locomotives, rolling stock and structures. Rutland cabooses had a more close family resemblance to NYC 19000-class cars, but the adoption of green and yellow colors made them look a bit more modern. While not a great enthusiast of freight operations, Gerrit knew that color could make the difference.
(Jeff English Collection)

127

(Above) Labor problems had shadowed the Rutland's future when Gerrit returned to the walkway leading to the Broadway Bridge. He sensed that there would only be a few more opportunities to photograph the Rutland's passage through Rensselaer. RS-3 #205 leads a mixed consist of freight headed for the Central interchange in Columbia County. The photo was taken in July of 1961, shortly before RC-4 was annulled due to the strike that terminated operations and the railway itself.

(Below) In May of 1960 Gerrit photographed northbound train CR-3 under the control of RS-3 #205. It is returning to its starting point in Rutland, a route which sees the train use B&A, NYC and B&M mainlines before hitting home rails at White Creek. From that point it only had to traverse the Rutland main line from North Bennington to Rutland before ending its run. The interchange with the NYC at Chatham provided a majority of the Rut's freight for a number of years. Today's train includes a gondola loaded with containers - probably bringing minerals up to Howe Scale. There they would be fed into Howe's small furnace to provide the steel needed for their scales. *(All, Jeff English Collection)*

(Below) Combine #260 brings up the markers just as it did for so many years on the Corkscrew Division. As it passes Tower 100 we see that the crew has made some small adjustments for their own comfort. The air conditioning remains just as was intended when the car was new - open windows at 30 MPH. The conductor is probably hard at work with the bills picked up from the B&A while the rear brakeman can be seen on the rear platform ready to acknowledge the tower operator's inspection of his train. Once again Gerrit proved how handy that walkway from the Broadway Bridge could be when photographing trains. And with this we bid adieu!

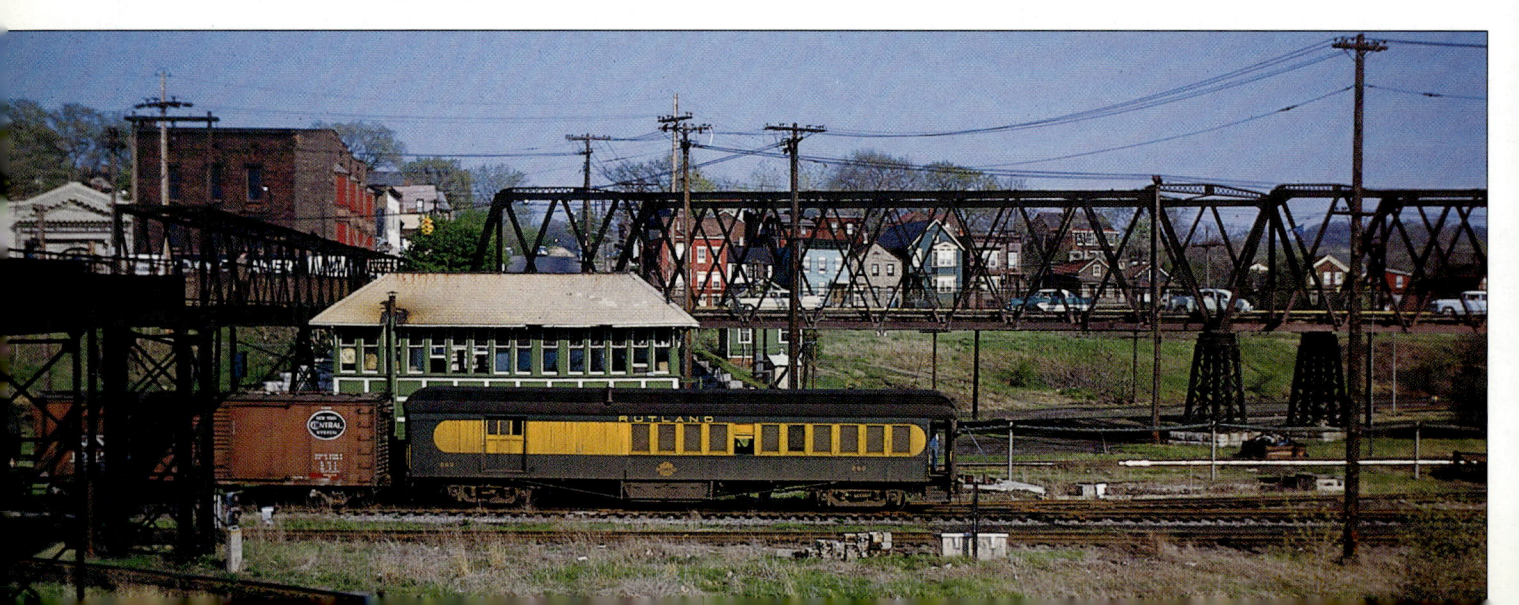